UNLOCK THE HIDDEN JOB MARKET

Praise for *Unlock the Hidden Job Market*

"Get the c̶ ̶̶̶̶̶̶̶̶ ̶̶̶̶̶̶̶̶̶̶ ̶̶̶ ̶̶̶̶̶̶̶̶ ̶̶̶̶̶̶̶̶ ̶̶̶̶ ̶̶̶̶̶̶̶̶ ̶̶̶̶̶̶ *Hidden* Job
Market \

—Marshall Goldsmith, executive c̶ ̶ ̶̶ and
Author of *What Got You Here Won't Get You There*

"Superb! All you need to guide you in finding that next career adventure!"

—Beverly Kaye, CEO/Founder, Career Systems International
and Author, *Love 'Em or Lose 'Em*

"Any active job seeker or individual considering a career change can benefit from Mathison and Finney's wisdom and practical advice. The great job search success stories today do not come from submitting one's resume among thousands of others, but from navigating unadvertised opportunities. It is precisely that hidden market that this book demystifies and opens for the reader."

—David Reimer, VP, North American Delivery,
Drake Beam Morin (DBM)

"When the economy is tight, finding a job takes a more proactive approach than simply responding to job ads with a good resume. Mathison and Finney tackle the art and science of finding good jobs that are never advertised and never posted on job boards."

—China Miner Gorman, Chief Operating Officer,
Society for Human Resource Management

"Great jobs are still out there! *Unlock The Hidden Job Market* gives you all the steps you need to find the perfect job for you. You can start today!"

—Rick Smith, Author of *The Leap!* and Founder of World 50, Inc.

"*Unlock the Hidden Job Market* gives you all the tools, insights, and strategies you need to take back the power of your job search. Mathison and Finney tell you exactly how to land not just any job, but the job that's perfect for you. Even now."

—Lauren Doliva, Managing Partner, Chief Advisor Network,
Heidrick & Struggles

"*Unlock the Hidden Job Market* shows you how to radically shift your perspective about your career potential. Need a new job? You need this book!"

—Libby Gill, executive coach and Author, *You Unstuck*

UNLOCK THE HIDDEN JOB MARKET

6 Steps to a Successful Job Search
When Times Are Tough

Duncan Mathison and Martha I. Finney

Vice President, Publisher: Tim Moore
Associate Publisher and Director of Marketing: Amy Neidlinger
Acquisitions Editor: Jennifer Simon
Editorial Assistant: Myesha Graham
Development Editor: Russ Hall
Operations Manager: Gina Kanouse
Senior Marketing Manager: Julie Phifer
Publicity Manager: Laura Czaja
Assistant Marketing Manager: Megan Colvin
Cover Designer: Alan Clements
Managing Editor: Kristy Hart
Project Editors: Julie Anderson and Jovana San Nicolas-Shirley
Copy Editor: Keith Cline
Proofreader: Sheri Cain
Indexer: Publishing Works Inc.
Compositor: Nonie Ratcliff
Manufacturing Buyer: Dan Uhrig

ISBN-10: 0-13-703249-8
ISBN-13: 978-0-13-703249-5

Pearson Education LTD.
Pearson Education Australia PTY, Limited.
Pearson Education Singapore, Pte. Ltd.
Pearson Education North Asia, Ltd.
Pearson Education Canada, Ltd.
Pearson Educación de Mexico, S.A. de C.V.
Pearson Education—Japan
Pearson Education Malaysia, Pte. Ltd.

Library of Congress Cataloging-in-Publication Data

Mathison, Duncan.
  Unlock the hidden job market : 6 steps to a successful job search when times are tough / Duncan Mathison and Martha I. Finney.
    p. cm.
  ISBN 978-0-13-703249-5 (pbk. : alk. paper) 1. Job hunting. 2. Job hunting—Computer network resources. 3. Employment interviewing. I. Finney, Martha I. II. Title.
  HF5382.7.M384 2010
  650.14—dc22
                          2009029510

*To my wife, Karen, and our daughters, Emily and Sarah.
No ship finds home port without her crew.*
—Duncan Mathison

Contents

Step 5: Get the Interviews That Count and Run Them Like a Pro — 149

Step 6: Negotiate Everything — 199

Acknowledgments

From Duncan:

The best gift anyone can offer is the introduction of professional people to one another. We often hear that the reason we need to network with people is to advance our own career. This can be so self-serving. It misses the point and gives networking a bad name. I cringe when I hear, "Hey there! How ya doin'? Say, I was wondering if you could introduce me to…." The real joy of networking comes when we make a connection between two people we think have similar values, compatible personalities, and synergistic talents. Where the introduction goes from there is up to them. Gift giving is an art. Some gifts end up in a drawer or the yard sale, while others hang on a wall. When lasting friendships and great enterprises are built on such introductions, everyone benefits.

Shari Fryer gave Martha and me just such a gift. As a marketing expert for professional services firms (www.fryerassociates.com), Shari knows more than her fair share of people. She took the time out of her busy schedule to introduce us because she thought we would be good coauthors. *Unlock the Hidden Job Market* would not have happened without you, Shari. From both of us, thank you.

Of course, a book like this works best when packed with really practical advice. And the best practical advice is gained only through experience of what flies and what flops. For this, I am grateful to the hundreds of jobseekers I worked with during my 18 years in the outplacement industry. Every day, they challenged me to come up with better ideas and taught me more than a few tricks of their own.

From Martha:

My thanks go to C.B.: Without you, this wouldn't have been half the fun or even a smidge as good. You made all the difference.

About the Authors

Duncan Mathison

For nearly 18 years, as Vice President, Managing Director, and Senior Consultant for DBM, an international outplacement, coaching, and career management firm, **Duncan Mathison** advised companies and their employees through reductions in force (RIFs), reorganizations, acquisitions, and operation shutdowns. For the employees impacted by job loss as a result of these actions, he has developed and delivered career transition strategies to help them rapidly find work in their field or successfully reinvent their careers. His clients have ranged across industries including finance, technology, telecommunications, biotechnology, retail, and entertainment.

Duncan is an author and speaker on organization performance, leadership, and executive career topics. He was a contributor to the three-volume book set *Building High-Performance People and Organizations* (Praeger, 2008) and an expert source in *Rebound: A Proven Plan for Starting Over After Job Loss,* by Martha I. Finney (FT Press, 2009). Mathison is frequently quoted on career and leadership issues in *The New York Times, The San Diego Union Tribune,* on CNN and MSNBC, as well as on online career advisors such as CareerBuilder.com and HotJobs.com.

Duncan Mathison may be reached at
Duncan@unlockthehidddenjobmarket.com.

Martha I. Finney

Martha I. Finney is President and CEO of Engagement Journeys, LLC, and an internationally respected expert in employee engagement and leadership communications. A business journalist for 20 years before becoming a full-time consultant, she specializes in helping organizations achieve greater employee loyalty, retention, and passion for their work. Her original research on the American workplace has been featured on CNN, NPR's *Morning Edition,* and major newspapers nationwide.

Finney is the author or coauthor of more than 14 books, which have been translated into 5 languages. Her most recent book is *Rebound: A Proven Plan for Starting Over After Job Loss* (FT Press, 2009).

Contact her at martha@reboundyourcareer.com. Follow Martha via twitter.com/marthafinney.

BREAK AWAY FROM THE HERD

CHAPTER 1

The Job Market Is Tight: It's Time to Take Back Control of Your Career

Great jobs don't go to great people. They go to great job searchers—those who know how to navigate the job market and make it work for them. Huge opportunities are waiting for you in the job market. Opportunities to not just find a great job in a really bad economy, but to build your career over time, on your terms, with your timing, and where you want to live and work.

There are actually two job markets. The one that everyone knows about—all those millions of job searchers who go to the same places and fight for a limited number of jobs that are published on job boards and online careers tabs on company websites. And then there is the hidden job market, that secret parallel universe of opportunities that are waiting for anyone with the skill, curiosity, and energy to seek them out. The *hidden job market* (HJM) is where you'll find your control. The hidden job market is where people are hired every day in jobs that are never published, never posted on the Internet, never put on the company website, nor listed in the newspaper, nor posted on job boards. The hidden job market is that vast source of opportunities where all jobs get their start, before some go on to be publicly announced, while others are just quietly filled with no official posting. This is where you have the competitive advantage, because you have found your own way there, through your own wits, initiative, and ingenuity. After you find the opportunity that's right for you, you can actually influence the design of that job, including the salary and benefits package that comes with it. That's the inside track that the hidden job market gives you. That's the control you're looking for.

Learning to navigate the hidden job market requires two things from you:

1. The willingness to take a more active role in your job search (which will be immediately more rewarding than sending out hundreds of resumés only to hear nothing from would-be employers).

2. The willingness to learn a new set of proven job search skills, which we call the HJM techniques, that you can put into *immediate* action (even today).

Sure, the HJM techniques will require more active effort from you, but it will be worth it! (You've probably already noticed that helplessly worrying is hard work, too. Wouldn't you rather invest your energies in activities that will actually land you a great job?)

How HJM Techniques Work

Here are some real-life examples of how the HJM techniques can help you reclaim control over your career (real people, names changed):

- **The HJM techniques help you get back on your career track.** John had early success in retail operations. When he was in his early 40s, he took a job with a computer company that wanted to open direct retail stores. The initiative failed, and he was let go. Using the HJM search techniques you'll learn in this book, he landed a job as vice president of operations for a specialty retailer, winning the job over two internal candidates whom the company president had been considering.

- **The HJM techniques can leapfrog you into a dream job without a perfect match of education, experience, or background.** Growing up on the wrong side of the tracks, Sarah followed her parents' wishes and went into business after college. But, despite a successful career in banking, she felt unfulfilled; she wanted to get into community service and help others make the leap to a better life, just as she had. The trouble was that those jobs required people with degrees in social work or public administration. She used the HJM techniques to discover what candidate characteristics really succeeded in those positions. Convincing the employer that she had those characteristics (the HJM techniques actually got her in front of the employer in the first place), she was able to demonstrate how her background made her the best candidate. She got the job over dozens of more qualified hopefuls.

- **The HJM techniques can help you find a job on your terms.** Edward worked for a company generating new ideas for the car industry, which he loves. He was quickly promoted to vice president, where he discovered that he hated the politics of management. He used the H JM techniques to create a portfolio of several high-quality part-time jobs, custom-created to allow him to do exactly what he loves to do. He's making more money than he ever did before. And he's happier now than he's ever been.

- **The HJM techniques can get you in the back door.** John specialized in a certain software programming language. But the market for that skill had dried up in Southern California, where he wanted to stay. He had burned out his network, and the online job boards turned up nothing. Using the HJM techniques, he found his next job in the most unlikely of places—his mother's church sewing circle. (So actually, it's more accurate to say that *she* used the HJM techniques.) A friend in the circle had a daughter who worked in a company that was looking for someone just like him. After getting over some initial, but terribly time-consuming, resistance against calling "the daughter of some church friend of Mom's," he discovered that this daughter worked in the division that needed him. He was hired within four days of making the call.

- **The HJM techniques can get you past the black hole of the applicant tracking system.** After spending a few years in high-tech, Bob wanted to return to the utilities industry, where he had spent the bulk of his early career. While he applied for a position through the conventional, published job route, he also used the HJM techniques to "get his foot in the door." He kept receiving automated rejection responses from the applicant tracking system, even while he was successfully negotiating with the exact same company a job offer he had received as a result of his HJM initiative.

- **The HJM techniques can transfer military experience into top corporate careers.** Paul, a Navy SEAL, didn't have to be told that the ability to land on beaches and blow things up was pretty much meaningless to the corporate world. He used the HJM techniques to identify the assets he did bring to the corporate world (innovation, the ability to get things done in highly uncertain environments, and building strong, cohesive teams). He also used the HJM techniques to bypass the automated applicant tracking system, which would have screened him out as having an irrelevant background. He went on to become a manager for a fast-track Fortune 500 company.

- **The HJM techniques can jump-start a dead job search.** Susan had been a highly respected specialist in organization development and was well networked in her town. After she was laid off, she had spent nine months and her entire severance combing through online job postings and conducting an unfocused, very expensive networking campaign. With only 30 days before she was due to lose her apartment (and move into her car), she launched an HJM search. She found a new job just in time, one that is perfect for her and pays more than what she earned in her previous job.

Maybe you see yourself in one of these people (or perhaps in bits of each). Or perhaps you have a different story—one that's making you ask yourself whether the HJM techniques can help you, too. These techniques will help no matter where you are in your career, even if you're just starting out or if you have reached the age where you think you might be too, uh, "overqualified" to be an attractive candidate. Maybe there are too many gaps in your resumé when you didn't have a paying job at all. (You were a mom or dad taking time off to be with the family, for instance. Or you were taking care of aging parents.) Or maybe you're thinking that you were one of your company's most highly paid employees when you were laid off. And now you wonder how you could possibly pick up that kind of income in a new position, especially when so many others are available and willing to work for less.

You can take control of your search in just six steps. Each step will increase your opportunities, sharpen your focus, and improve your chances for that hard-to-come-by dream opportunity that will actually turn into an offer. Each step answers the most difficult questions of any job search and puts you in control and on the path to successful employment:

Step 1: Make Five Mindset Fixes to Get Your Search on Track identifies five mindsets to help you avoid the most common assumptions that derail any job search. This essential step answers

- How to measure whether you are on track in your search or just wasting your time

- Why being between jobs is actually an advantage when you conduct an HJM search
- How just a 30-minute daily investment of your time will actually shorten your job search
- Why hiring managers will choose to hire you over someone else when you don't have the exact experience they want

Step 2: Connect Your Hottest Skills to What Hiring Managers Really Care About shows you how to identify which skills will actually get you hired. In addition, this important assessment step tells you

- How to overcome a career setback caused by losing your job
- How to transfer your current skills to new industries and professions
- Practical steps to overcome experience gaps that stand between you and your dream job

Step 3: Upgrade Your Networking to Get Better Results will break you free of unproductive networking ruts and enable you to finally do networking right. This step shows you

- Why you're better off just skipping those expensive, fattening, and boring networking mixers.
- How to talk about yourself and your goals without sounding phony, lame, or desperate
- How to focus on the best networking opportunities
- How you will know that your networking is working and not just wasting your time

Step 4: Power Up Your Job Search gives you a new set of tools to organize and focus your search. These tools will transform and energize your search when you learn

- Why you should leave your resumé at home

- How to create a document more powerful than a resumé that will open doors, generate ideas, and ultimately introduce you to the person who will offer you your job
- How to find the perfect job exactly where you want to live
- How to discover the hot industry issues that create the hot new jobs

Step 5: Get the Interviews That Count and Run Them Like a Pro is a practical guide to get inside a target employer and conduct a powerful HJM meeting. You will learn

- How to get an appointment with the people who have the power to actually hire you
- How to discover specific job opportunities during an HJM meeting
- The secret to being treated like an accomplished professional instead of just another out-of-work applicant
- How to move an HJM meeting toward a job offer

Step 6: Negotiate Everything teaches you to get the most of any job offer by explaining

- How to custom-write your own job description
- When and how to nudge the hiring manager into making an offer
- How to negotiate *both* the salary and job title that you deserve

This book is about bringing the best of who you are to the best selection of job opportunities that are out there. It's not about playing games, having the absolutely perfect resumé, being phony, being ashamed, or being desperate. It is about being authentic, being confident, being curious, and matching your abilities, skills, and desires with the right job—with the compensation you deserve.

No matter what you think your barriers are to your next great job, the HJM techniques can work for you and put you back in control of your career and your future. If you follow the advice in this book, you will unlock doors you didn't even know existed, or that maybe you assumed were closed to you. The hidden job market approach is a journey where you will discover new possibilities and opportunities.

The best thing you can do:
Resolve to take back control of your career.

The worst thing you can do:
Let yourself become so overwhelmed by the frustrations that go with traditional job search methods that you just give up.

The first thing you should do:
Open your mind to the possibilities that these proven HJM techniques will help you land your next great job and reclaim both your career and your future.

CHAPTER 2

Don't Trust the Official "System": It's Not Working in Your Favor

Depending on who you are and what your particular dreams are, you probably have a list of companies that you would love to work for. Perhaps any one of the 100 companies on *Fortune*'s annual Best Companies to Work For list? Or even the runners-up would be nice. Or maybe any one of the Working Mother-endorsed companies? Or AARP-endorsed companies? Or maybe your tastes run toward the more adventurous: Wouldn't it be great to work for one of those luxury cruise lines that take passengers on eco-aware journeys to the Galapagos?

It's probably not hard to create a list of your ideal companies. The trouble is, how do people get inside? Surely there has to be a system. Some of these companies employ tens of thousands of very lucky people. If you happen to live near their headquarters, you know this for a personal fact. You've seen their parking lots full of cars. All those lucky cars, with their lucky drivers happily working away in a collegial spirit of focusing their time, energy, smarts, and skills on a shared goal. For a company that is magnificently managed and is the leader in its field.

How do you get your foot in the door? Which door, for that matter? What is that one door that is set up for stone-cold outsiders, such as yourself, who only ask for a chance to be noticed and considered? And then perhaps invited in for an interview. Followed by, of course, the offer of a great job because you are just as capable as the people they have. With all those thousands of employees already on the payroll, the company must have an elegant system, a process by which to find people just like you, who are at the right place at the right time with just the right skill sets. Surely. Right?

Nope. Well… let's rephrase that a little bit. The company of your dreams may have a process, but that doesn't necessarily mean it's working. And that certainly doesn't mean it's working for you. In fact, it could be working against you. Not intentionally, of course. But the results are still the same.

The idea of a company having a sophisticated, smoothly run, imminently fair process for seeking, finding, and recruiting ideal talent (that would be you) is a modern myth supported by the whiz-bang of technology. In fact, the employers' pursuit of mass-efficiency over the last couple of decades has resulted in bringing in more resumés rather than welcoming any individual superior candidate who especially wants to work for a particular company for specific reasons (that would be you).

From the perspective of individual applicants who really, really, really want to work for a specific company, getting a job is a messy, disorganized, haphazard process. True, people do get hired in the conventional job search process, using companies' established recruiting systems. However, the conventional job search process is still too much a matter of dumb luck and timing. And isn't your career too important to rely on dumb luck and timing?

Here are some of the ways the "system" (assuming there is one) can fail you:

- **Even companies with sophisticated recruitment processes have haphazard ways of finding the best talent.** Individual internal recruiters deal in volume. They tend to be used when there is a shortage of applicants, and they are often entry-level HR people. For many positions, particularly higher-level positions, they are simply bypassed. They set up database systems into which they dump unsolicited resumés and create automated responses: "Thank you for your interest in our company…." When recruiting slows, internal recruiters are often among the first employees to lose their jobs. Managers are left on their own to find people, and they often outsource searches for candidates when they do need to hire. External recruiters may struggle under the disadvantage of not having a deep understanding of the company culture or that extra special something that will make the candidate the best fit for the hiring manager. The hiring managers themselves might not know exactly what they want. And if you rely on the conventional ways of getting in the door, you drastically reduce your chances of brainstorming the future with the person who could be your fantastic next boss.

- **Only a small fraction of open positions are even published.** However, 100% of all positions are "hidden" at some point (most likely in the very early stages of their development, when you can have the most influence over how those job descriptions are written). But once they're published—*if* they're published—you could get lost in the stampeding desperation of millions of other job seekers who just want a job (any job, please! please! please!).

  So isn't it to your advantage to get ahead of the herd? Tap into jobs before they are published, and you'll have a greater selection and less competition, if any.

- **The drive to somehow stand apart from that crowd could compel you to try truly goofy gimmicks.** *Do not* attach your resumé to a bouquet of balloons. Or attach it to a Starbucks gift card. Or send it via singing messenger. You don't want to stand out by looking stupid. You want to stand out by being extraordinary, and by having the right person notice how extraordinary you are. Using the HJM techniques will position you in that perfect light.

- **Conventional job searching methods, and recruitment systems, begin (and end) with resumés.** Resumés are a necessary evil, but they are not your friend. They give people reasons to screen you out more than welcome you in for further discussion. Resumés are about your past. The job search is about your future. And the company's future. And how you can help each other get there.

  Using the HJM techniques, your introduction to a potential employer is much better than a resumé, and certainly more dignified than a singing messenger (no offense to all you singing messengers out there). You are in control of the way you introduce yourself and your talents to the company you might want to work for. You decide whom you call (and you're not waiting for someone to call you), who introduces you to whom, and what the tone is of that first one-on-one meeting.

  When you're using the HJM techniques, you are a person in the mind of the hiring manager, not just a piece of paper. It's a snap to toss aside a two-page resumé, especially when thousands of others just like it are waiting to be read and screened. But in the hidden job market, you're *right there*, a real human being talking to the hiring manager. And you're not so easy to thoughtlessly dismiss, especially when you're conducting the HJM meeting, driving the quality of the conversation.

- **Applicant tracking systems are designed to spit you out.** You could be the perfect candidate for the published job. But: you're competing with hundreds of applicants whose resumé keywords might be just a bit more perfect. You know that there are many jobs that you can do, transferring completely appropriate skills from one industry to another. But: because your resumé doesn't have the exact keyword matches, as compared with the next person's, you're placed at the bottom of the list or spit out of the system altogether.

You know you can do the job, and you may be even more motivated than the "perfect candidate" with all the right keyword matches. But: the applicant tracking system isn't programmed to pick out your passion.

- **The savvy hiring managers are already circumventing the official "system," assuming there is one.** No one is better positioned to know how flawed the internal recruitment system is. Rightly or wrongly, the more powerful senior leaders won't even bring HR into the recruitment discussion, especially if that open position is at a higher level than their HR director. Some may use executive search firms. But that represents a significant expense (up to 30% of your first year's salary), one that many companies are loath to take on right now.

So what do these hiring managers do? They tap into the hidden job market: their friends; their professional networks; their resources; total strangers who call them and ask for a few minutes' time to get acquainted and discuss their profession, business, or company.

Using the HJM techniques, you're also circumventing the so-called official "system." You have something in common with the hiring manager already. And because you're not waiting for the applicant tracking system to miraculously discover you, you've found other ways into the companies of your choice, having one-on-one meetings with people who might be in a position to hire you (or who might know someone who is). While the recruiting department (if there still is one) is busily shuffling through applications, you're already sitting in front of the hiring manager. You're right there. Which puts you in a perfect position to demonstrate that you're a really pleasant individual who not only has the ability to get the job done, but also has that extra special spark to get the job done beautifully.

That's the spark that will get you the job offer. The HJM system is the system that works. That's the system you should use. Because it's the system you control.

The best thing you can do:
Let go of any expectation that the way companies recruit is orderly, sensible, and fair.

The worst thing you can do:
Spend money on some executive agency that promises to "get you in the door" of hiring companies. No one will represent you better than you.

The first thing you should do:
Start a list of every organization you think would hire someone with your skills (even if you think they might have a hiring freeze).

Three Strikes Do Not Count as an Out

After several years working as a test engineer for a utility company, Bob decided that it was time to update his career and focus on high tech—specifically, sophisticated computer chips, semiconductors, and networks. But the semiconductor industry has its ups and downs, and in a downturn, he was quickly out of a job. With a family to support and a new mortgage, Bob wanted to get back into the utilities, where he would have more job security. He applied for every job that was posted at the nearby gas and electric company.

He got a polite note from Human Resources: "Thank you for your application. All applications are under review and we will contact you in the future for an interview if your skills match our needs." *Strike one.* He applied for another position in the same company. Same response. *Strike two.* Now Bob was really running out of time. After applying for a third position, he called a former co-worker to renew their acquaintance. He, in turn, arranged a networking meeting for Bob with a manager.

A week later, the manager called him back and introduced him to an internal group that was looking for someone with precisely his blend of skills and experience.

Later that day, the manager told him, "They want to put together an offer." Bob was thrilled. But the next day, he got yet another automated rejection notice from Human Resources: "After reviewing your qualifications, we have concluded we have no positions for you at this time." He was crushed. *Strike three.*

Two days later, the manager called back. "We have an offer for you. When can you start?"

Bottom line: Bob got hired for a job that was never published; never went through Human Resources; was never officially in the system. The formal system rejected him not once, but three times. And he still got the job.

STEP 1

MAKE FIVE MINDSET FIXES TO GET YOUR SEARCH ON TRACK

CHAPTER 3

Stay Home or Stay in Control: Beliefs That Can Kill Your Job Search

When you're just beginning to consider the HJM search as a possible approach to finding your next job, it might feel like it's a large, shapeless mass of possibilities surrounded by a maze of dead-ends and a tangle of unreturned, cold, phone calls. The "system" of published job opportunities seems so seductively organized and automated (and we've already established that that's not the case) that it's tempting to just sit back and let the world's network of computers talk to each other and spit out an interview appointment for you—for that one great appointment that will net you that one great job offer. All you need to do is just comb the online job boards and then wait for your number to come up.

That's like the overwhelming desire to fall asleep in the snow when you're freezing to death. Don't do it.

True, pursuing the hidden job market (HJM) takes a lot of initiative (just when all you want to do is take that nap); tolerance for ambiguity (just when all you want is a little certainty in your life, is that too much to ask?); the courage to seek out and meet highly successful people (just when the last thing you heard at work might have been, "I'm afraid we're going to have to let you go"); and patience (just when you need a job *now*).

But the hidden job market *is* the place you're looking for. It gives you that control you crave. And, as you will see throughout the rest of this book, it is highly organized, and much of it is very predictable. But still…there are some common assumptions about the hidden job market that might make you feel like now is a good time for a little shut-eye. Let's see if we can dispel them and get you on track for finding the right job for you.

Assumption 1: The HJM is about getting lucky.

Actually, as we've already discussed, the time you need luck the most is when you're depending on the traditional published channels to find and land a job. Blasting out resumés to long-shot job ads is like buying a lottery ticket. It only marginally improves your chances of winning. In the hidden job market, you're the one in control.

But if you go after the HJM using search techniques that we'll be teaching you, you drive your own luck. You get to decide whom you want to meet, and *you'll* be the one to pick up the phone to make meetings happen. Of course, not everyone will be willing to meet with you (there will be a rejection ding every now and then, we won't kid you), but you'll have many more meetings this way than you would if you were just passively waiting for a busy HR department to finally get around to considering your resumé—perhaps weeks after you clicked "submit " in response to the online posting. If ever.

Assumption 2: Because I have to do everything myself, the HJM takes more time than the published job market.

So? What else do you have going on? Picking up the dry cleaning? Retiling the bathroom? Packing the kids' lunches? Desperately catching up on all those premium-channel movies before you cancel your cable service? We're not telling you to abandon the published job market. But let's face it, you can do that research in just a few hours a week. And then you have the leisure of spending the rest of the week worrying about not finding a new job, while distracting yourself with errands and life's little annoyances.

If you were too busy to get around to those things while you had a full-time job, you don't have time to do those now. You can be using those hours profitably to find the right job with the right company on your terms. Isn't that a better way to invest all that time on your hands? This is about return on your investment, after all.

Assumption 3: Because HJM research conversations aren't directed at any particular job opening, I'd just be shooting the breeze during those interviews.

As you will see later in this book, these HJM research conversations (they're not interviews) are very organized, with an extremely specific agenda. They're specifically designed to trigger brainstorming, give you more insight into your industry or profession, and generate more introductions. This is not about creating bonding opportunities by comparing notes on news, weather, and sports. It's about using great HJM research conversations to drive your powerful job search.

Each HJM conversation will enrich you with exactly what you need to push your search campaign forward.

Assumption 4: Outsiders don't get HJM jobs, only insiders do.

True, plenty of job opportunities are filled from within. (After all, that day-to-day, relationship- and reputation-building opportunity really is a great networking advantage.) But that doesn't mean you're shut out from all job opportunities that are right for you. Especially these days, when so much in the world is struggling to abandon outdated or dysfunctional practices of the past to create more promising futures.

Organizations of all kinds (businesses, government agencies, nonprofits) are looking for fresh ideas and better ways to achieve their objectives. So they are especially open to bringing great thinking in from the outside. This is where you might have the advantage.

Assumption 5: Nobody's going to want to talk to me; they're too busy.

No, they aren't too busy to meet and hire valuable talent who will make them successful. That's one of the core responsibilities for managers. The good ones know that. Those are the ones you want to talk with anyway.

When you're between jobs, it's natural to let your self-talk tempt you into believing that the people you want to talk with have more valuable things to do with their time than talk with you. But, in fact, as you start getting really good at running HJM conversations, you'll discover that they're thanking *you* for the meeting and for all the ideas that the two of you generated. You're doing them a favor as much as you are driving a job search campaign. You'll quickly start believing that with a few of these HJM research meetings under your belt.

Assumption 6: It's not polite to apply for a job that's not officially published.

No one is going to be offended if you come into their work world and solve their problem for them. If there is an identified need that has been turned into a defined job that must be filled, you've just saved the hiring manager hours, days, weeks, and even months of time finding you (not to mention thousands of dollars in recruitment costs). And if the need hasn't yet been turned into a job opening, no one yet owns the task of filling that opening. Therefore, no one will be in a snit because you did some sort of "end-run" around his or her turf.

Finally, should someone be offended that you overstepped some political sensitivity by just having an authentic HJM conversation with one of the company's managers, that could be a sign that the organizational culture is full of political landmines. This is an important data point for you to keep in mind when considering whether the company is really for you.

Assumption 7: Nobody's going to want to talk to me if I'm out of work.

If you're between jobs because you were laid off or fired, the last message you received from your previous employer was a variation of the following: "What you have to offer is no good to us." That's a nice blow to your confidence, isn't it? Compound that with loss of title, place on an org chart, business card with an established company's logo on it (rather than one of those print-it-yourself jobs that you can spot a mile away), combined with all that time on your hands to stew about your misfortune, and what you have is confidence crisis. Just when you need your confidence the most, that's when it's the most hammered.

But when you go out into the hidden job market, you start seeing your value as a professional beyond the context of the company that rejected you. The HJM search techniques give you the chance to discover the way others see your gifts as being important to them regardless of what might have happened in the past. In fact, because *you* will be driving the HJM research conversation, the matter of your past might not even come up until much later. If at all.

People will want to talk with you because you're a peer (a colleague, an equal) exploring professional possibilities. You're not an applicant begging for work and forcing them to make a thumbs-up/thumbs-down decision.

Assumption 8: It takes more effort to find a job this way than to rely on the established job search process.

That would be true. More effort, but less time until you land. Besides, how hard is it to feel powerless and stress about the lack of job opportunities out there—envisioning all sorts of dread scenarios for you and your family? You are going to have to exert effort one way or the other. Relying only on the published job market will squander your time. Your return on that investment? A feeling of hopelessness and loss of professional value.

Or you can take back your career. Take a proactive approach to driving a search campaign that could generate not just one option, but perhaps multiple offers. You will meet people you will want to know, have fascinating and valuable conversations that will grow your contacts, and learn more about your profession, industry, or community. Instead of using your considerable intellect to tear yourself apart for being out of work and not being able to attract prospective employers, you are going out there to seek the people with whom you really need to be talking.

If you are a curious person and want to learn about your professional world and career prospects, the HJM approach will help you use your time to benefit yourself, to discover new and exciting ways your skills meet the needs of your industry or community.

Keep your mind open to all the possibilities that will reveal themselves in the hidden job market. And soon, as you begin to connect the dots, a picture of your true prospects will emerge, and you'll clearly see your next best opportunities.

The best thing you can do:
If your old company gave you an outplacement or career transition package to help you with the job search, take advantage of it.

The worst thing you can do:
Blindly send your resumé to search firms and expect that they will do the job searching and door opening for you.

The first thing you should do:
Create an action plan. Update it every weekend for the coming week. Remember that you are in control of this search.

"I Will Not Beg for a Job"

Success and promotions had always come easily for David. He started his career with a major aerospace firm straight out of college, and company executives quickly recognized his talent, his intelligence, and his commitment. Promotions soon followed, until he reached the peak of his career as vice president of finance. But when the company was sold, the new owners wanted to put their own leadership team in place. Now, for the first time in his life, David was unemployed and, unfortunately, burdened with misplaced, damaged pride. To him, networking was the same as begging. And, despite his extensive accomplishments and his connections on Wall Street, he would not budge from what he believed to be his last remaining shred of dignity. "I will not beg for a job," he would say. He could not even bring himself to call people who respected his talents the most, knew he would be a valuable asset to any company, and cared about him personally. It wasn't being laid off that wrecked his career. It was his insistent resistance to network.

CHAPTER 4

The HJM Search Is a Different Kind of Numbers Game

Even when the economy is flourishing, when you are out of work and looking for a new job, it's hard to keep your spirits up, especially when you're just going after publicly posted jobs. You've got a lot of time on your hands, and you spend that time frittering, clicking "Submit" on online applications, worrying, or most likely, all three. It's nerve-wracking, to be sure. But at least you can take some comfort in knowing that, in a thriving job economy, *some* employer will eventually get around to you. It's not the most efficient way to target a job, but at least you know the numbers are on your side.

Now, when the economy is sloughing off livelihoods, like it's doing as we're writing this book, the numbers feel like your enemy. When upward of a million jobs are disappearing every month around the world, that means three things to you: fewer companies are hiring, fewer established jobs are available, and your competition for those jobs has just increased by seven digits. That doesn't feel very hopeful, especially when the process of finding a job isn't exactly set up like a deli where all you have to do is pull a number and holler, "Hey! I was here first!," when someone tries to cut in line in front of you. So what if you've already been waiting (and worrying) for three, five, six months, and now you're joined by a million new desperate faces?

It's hard not to take the mounting numbers of jobless folks as a personal threat to your place in line. But in your job search, especially if you are mastering the hidden job market (HJM), it's not about scrambling with any of those millions of people for the scattering of measly jobs that have been tossed into the marketplace. It's about calmly and systematically going about your own targeted job search, heedless of the frustrated efforts of your fellow unemployed—unless, in your networking activities, you uncover an opportunity that's perfect for someone you know. The hidden job market isn't about being selfish, it's about being focused. And not letting the economic agonies distract or demoralize you from your mission.

Former executives walking Madison Avenue wearing sandwich boards announcing their availability for work. Architects manning crafts fair stands, peddling home rehab advice, like Lucy charging 5 cents for psychological help in the comic strip *Peanuts*. Hundreds of resumés for one high school janitor job. Parents competing with their teenagers for summer jobs at the local theme park. The bad news isn't meant for you. If you're tempted to think, "Who am I to hope for a great job when all these other talented people are out of work, too?," you'll be thrown off your game.

People who don't know any better will say that finding a job is a numbers game. What they mean by that is that the more resumés you fling out into cyberworld, the better your chances are of landing a new job. And they would be wrong about that. You can send out thousands of resumes, but if they just land in a heap with thousands of other resumés, you're not improving your odds at all. In fact, you may be just improving your chances of staying unemployed.

The hidden job market is a numbers game, but they are different kinds of numbers:

- **Millions of unemployed people.** Don't let the headlines overwhelm you. You're not competing with everyone who is looking for a job. Let them compete with each other while you go about your business of finding the job you want. Ignore them.

- **200 organizations.** As you go through your HJM research, you will be compiling a list of organizations that could conceivably hire people like you.

- **85–100 people.** Get outside of your immediate professional community and neighborhood. Start your list with everyone you know, even though they may be outside your profession. Those people might be able to shed light on your search in ways you've never considered, giving you insight into your industry, profession, and colleagues.

- **5–8 meetings.** When you conduct the HJM search, you can have five to eight meetings a week. They're not job interviews, per se. Nor are they just networking schmoozing. But some of them could conceivably turn into interviews. Even if they don't, they're still valuable to your search process. You will meet new people who have fresh ideas for you and introduce you to yet more people—one of whom will eventually be the one to hire you.

- **5–10 opportunities.** Eventually, you will have a short list of job possibilities that you think could be actual matches for your abilities and search objectives.

- **3 offers.** You want at least three viable offers that match all your requirements for your next career step. When you have your pick of three viable offers, you can select the best of the three. And if, for some reason, it doesn't pan out, you've got two backups. You're still in control of your destiny.

- **1 job.** Unless you are going after a portfolio career where you are fitting together multiple, high-level but part-time jobs (which the HJM search techniques can help you with as well), all you want is one full-time job.

Other than the first category, these are the numbers you should focus on. They are completely within your control. They have nothing to do with the dread labor statistics published every month. And they have everything to do with your initiative and how well you invest your job search time.

There's one more number that you should keep in mind: Your emotional well-being (of which you have one). Protect it at all costs while you learn to explore the hidden job market. Focusing on the bleakness of the job market will overwhelm you. And when you're overwhelmed, your energy diminishes and your capacity for creative thinking plummets.

Stop watching the news (or at least the economic news, but what else is out there these days?) for the time that you're driving your search campaign. If you have friends who indulge in "ain't it awful" conversations, put them on notice that you won't be participating for the time being. You're not being Alfred E. Neuman ("What, me worry?") or Scarlett O'Hara ("I'll think about that tomorrow"), you're just ferociously protecting your peace of mind while you take on what could be the most important adventure of your professional life.

Sure, you might miss some important headlines. Right now, the world doesn't need you to stay on top of breaking news as much as *you* need you to take care of yourself to achieve your job goals. You can catch up later.

And build in time to have fun. This is more than just balance in life (which is pretty important in and of itself). It's about taking care of your capacity to think clearly and creatively. Harvard researchers have linked play with break-through problem solving. As it turns out, there's nothing like having a good time today to facilitate a "eureka" tomorrow.

So. Have a good time while you look for just one job. The job that's right for you.

The best thing you can do:
Remember that opportunities come into the marketplace every day, as people leave jobs to take new ones, others start new businesses, new industries emerge, and new funding is committed for important projects.

The worst thing you can do:
Take up residence in Pity City.

The first thing you should do:
Keep working on that list of 100 people. We'll tell you what to do with them later.

The 100th Time Was the Charm

Alan moved to San Diego from New York City. Unemployment in San Diego was 7%, and the beaches were a lot warmer than the economy. He knew no one in his new hometown, but was determined to make his new home and new life in San Diego anyway. He loved public relations and communications but saw few ads for jobs in those fields. So Alan decided he would create a list of 100 people he knew and contact them to ask if they would introduce him to anyone they might know in San Diego. The first 35 names were easy. From 35 to 80, he had to dig through his parents' connections and even some old high school buddies. The last 20 were brutal. The 100th person on his list was a guy he worked with while in college as a runner on the floor of the New York Stock Exchange. The 100th person knew only one person in San Diego. And that person hired Alan in his first investor relations job that launched his sunny San Diego career.

CHAPTER 5

You Don't Have to Have a Job to Get a Job

It wasn't that long ago when the general assumption was that already having a job was your strongest position for shopping for a new one. In fact, your friends would discourage you from quitting a nightmare job because being unemployed presumably weakened you in the marketplace. In other words, "What are you? Some kind of a loser? Can't keep a job?"

Maybe it's human nature, but if you are already employed elsewhere, potential employers might think you are a catch to steal from someone else (ideally, their competition). You are "in demand," you are "valued" by someone else. So that must mean you are a talent that must be snatched up—preferably yesterday, if not sooner.

Also, when you're already drawing a bimonthly paycheck that meets your needs, and you're relatively happy where you are, you can walk into a job interview with a sense of detachment that reads cool, calm, and collected. You're not desperate for a new job. The prospect of living in your car isn't looming large and dreadful. You're fine. You're just there out of leisurely curiosity and maybe the possibility of improving your lot.

Or so the thinking goes. But the reality never works that way, does it? If you buy into the belief that current employment is key to your desirability for a new position, you're handicapping yourself in the current marketplace.

Actually, the beauty of the hidden job market (HJM) is that you're actually better off *unemployed* while you're conducting your search. Here's what you have going for you as an individual "presently at liberty":

- **The hidden job market search will take you much less time to complete if you devote your full time to it.** Sure, you can do a hidden job market search while holding down a full-time job, but instead of taking only three to five months to find just the right job that matches your talents and skills, it could take you as long as a year or even more to pull it off. We're not suggesting that you quit a perfectly good job to pursue the idea of something potentially better. But we are suggesting that you see the benefits of being on your own as a way to speed up your process significantly.

- **You don't have to worry about getting busted.** Let's face it, word gets out. And some bosses actually devote their own precious time searching job boards for the names of their employees to see who might be out there looking. (Any boss who has time to skulk around the job boards in this way would be better off using that time to take training or read books on how to be a better boss.) Even worrying about getting caught is distracting and energy-draining. And you need all your resources to explore possibilities as fully as you can.

   When you're already unemployed, you can navigate the hidden job market openly, with no games and no subterfuge. And that openness is crucial in the hidden job market. The more people know that you're out there looking, the more likely it is that one of them will introduce you to the person who will introduce you to the person who will ask you, "When can you start?"

- **Your identity belongs to you.** When you're working for another company, you take the baggage with that company with you on your job search. (Think Enron, AIG, and Madoff Investment Securities.) Not every company is burdened with headline-making shame or embarrassment, of course. But even within small business communities, there might be relationships between companies that could be to your disadvantage. When you're your own representative, you're there to talk about a mutually beneficial future, not a dinged or damaged past of some aspect of your organization that you had nothing to do with.

- **You can devote all your time and energy to driving your search campaign.** The hidden job market is best explored when you can focus all your energy and attention on exploring possibilities. Squeezing crucial HJM research meetings into your busy working days will only dilute your efforts and prolong the process. It can be done if you have a full-time job already, but you can reach your goals much faster as a free agent.

You also have the time you need to research companies, industries and professions you want to consider for this new phase of your life. This is the time to put yourself in learning mode—an opportunity that you might not have had time for in your busy past.

- **You have more time for the self-discovery needed to find the job (and subsequent career path) that's right for you.** The HJM search is shorter than doing a traditional search approach alone after you know what you really want to do. Yet an essential aspect of the hidden job market is your willingness to be curious and open-minded. When you're doing this while holding down a demanding job, you might not be as open to the time-consuming exploration adventure as you need to be to really get the most out of the hidden job market. This process can take more time on a daily basis to explore avenues that might turn into dead ends for you. If you are rushed, trying to fit this process within a full plate of work responsibilities, you might be tempted to shortcut the discovery process. You might be tempted to prejudge some of those avenues of exploration as not worth your time, when those might be the very avenues that hold some amazing surprises for you.

- **You bring very real advantages to a new employer when you are currently unemployed.** Your answer to "When can you start?" can be "Right away." Your new employer can have you now. There is no need to wait the two weeks' or month's notice period. There is no current employer who might extend a counteroffer to you. There is no concern that you might suffer buyer's remorse and try to boomerang back to your old job. There is no old job to boomerang back to. Your new employer doesn't have to worry that you might be a quitter or a job-hopper, especially if you were laid off from your last job.

Flexibility, availability, focus and independence—these are just a few reasons why having a job does not create a significant advantage over people who don't have jobs.

The best thing you can do:
Come to terms with being unemployed. Good people, really good people, lose their jobs every day because of economic forces beyond their control.

The worst thing you can do:
Obsess about your separation from your previous employer. If you find yourself ruminating, gently give yourself permission to let it go

The first thing you should do:
Write a positive statement about the circumstances surrounding your job loss that will play well in an interview.

> ## "Enough Games. I Need Someone to Start Now!"
>
> After an intense full-time search, Susan interviewed for a director of organizational development job at a fast-growing company. The week before, the company had already offered that job to another candidate, who decided to stay with her previous employer. "The manager told me they had wasted weeks recruiting this person and after extensive negotiations of salary and perks, the job candidate simply used their offer to get a raise and promotion at her current company. He asked me if I could start right away so he could get me involved in the team's offsite meeting starting Sunday night. I said yes, and he made me an offer on the spot with a full relocation package!"

CHAPTER 6

Make Your Passion Your Most Competitive Asset

If you've been in the work world for any length of time (even if you've just left your first job), the chances are excellent that you have been told by at least one person that pursuing your passion is all very nice, but it won't put bread on the table. It's almost as if the mere fact that you have a passion about something automatically disqualifies it as a viable career path. Expressions like "castles in the air" or terms such as "pipedreams" immediately come into play when you talk about some kind of work or life experience that makes your eyes light up.

We go to work for a variety of rewards, the paycheck being just one of them. And, if we're healthy and hopeful, our real ambition is to build a body of work over our lifetime that allows us to express the best of who we are in a way that we can actually be paid for it. We grow and change over the years, perhaps even changing our values and perspectives. But, when we're so busy "holding down a job," we forget to keep up with ourselves and track what passions have endured over the years, what we've grown out of, and what we've grown into without realizing it. The hidden job market (HJM) search begins with rediscovering (or discovering for the first time) who you have become since you took your first job at, say, 18. (Think about how much you've changed. And consider this: Would you allow the 18-year-old you used to be drive your car now? Well, just think about how much you're letting that 18-year-old drive your career based on a set of decisions you made way back then.)

If you abandoned your particular life's passion in favor of pursuing a more "realistic" approach to building your career, you might have also abandoned your true competitive edge—that sparkle in your eye. When hiring managers consider a selection of equally qualified candidates for a position, they commonly assume that 20% of their team is going to drive 80% of the team's performance. If the measurable qualifications are equal, what's going to give a person that 20% advantage? Passion for the gig. So, why continue to ignore that one aspect of your total package that could put you ahead of all the rest in terms of your ability to perform the job on an extraordinary level? One important answer is that, in a traditional search process (job search for you and talent search for the hiring manager), the subject of passion rarely comes up. While we may sometimes see the description buried in a job listing, the emphasis is on your skills and experience. Consequently, any potential conversation about what really puts performance in that top 20% category recedes into the far distance, while you and your interviewer focus intently on your past track record.

In contrast, the hidden job market search is largely about your passion and how you can turn it into non-negotiable must-haves for you and an irresistible must-have for a collection of carefully selected companies that you have identified as a great fit. But, if you have had a career history of tamping down that passion in service of the day-to-day humdrum of getting and doing a job, you might need help to reconnect with that core ingredient that really puts the spark in your eye. Over the years of your career so far, many layers of self-denial, false steps, ignored yearnings, and even new discoveries have built up around some essential aspects of who you are and what you can really bring to the table. You have gotten great at fitting yourself in a job rather than identifying the job that would be a good fit for you and then holding out for it. If you've gotten into the habit of squeezing yourself into wrong fits over the course of a few years, or even a few decades, you're going to need some help returning to yourself. Not just to the young version of the unmitigated you just starting out in the work world (when you might not have been too shy to say, "What I'd really like to do is..."), but also to the authentic, seasoned you who has since discovered new interests, previously unknown ways the world works, and all the different ways you can combine your passions with your skills to really shine in your work.

When you go through the extra effort of combing through the hidden job market for the next step on your career path, you owe it to yourself to make certain that that next step is the right one.

And that's where the power of journaling comes in. This is not about dreaming, "Gee, I'd like to train unicorns for a traveling road show for well-behaved children everywhere." (Let's be real here, how many children are that well behaved?) It's about confronting the essential you, what you really want out of life and work. And it's even about getting past some anger that's keeping you from moving toward the right future.

The effectiveness of this approach has been documented. In the early 1990s, two researchers, J. W. Pennebaker (University of Texas) and Stephanie Spera (a psychologist with an outplacement firm) assembled a group of men who had been laid off in a city that was suffering extremely high unemployment. All of these guys had already been in the search process for four months. The researchers asked half the study group to write about their thoughts and feelings about the layoff and job search for 30 minutes a day for 5 consecutive days. The other half was simply assigned to document how they used their time during this same period. (A separate group—a control group—did not write at all during this time. Too bad for them.) The results of the study showed that those who processed through their feelings (especially the anger part) via their journaling projected more promise in job interviews. Within a few months, more than half of the group that journaled had landed jobs. But only 18% of those who didn't journal had found employment by that time. And get this: They'd all had the same number of interviews.

By the time the study concluded, the researchers found that those who journaled were three times more likely to land jobs within the time frame of the study itself. So, there has to be something to this journaling idea. At the least, it's a great way to capture what your true passions are in both life and work. Clients who have worked with Duncan discover that after cooperating with his suggestion to start journaling, they end up with a clearer sense of what is important to them, what their priorities are (and in what order), what they really did like about their previous jobs (and of course, what they didn't). This clarity of purpose, ability to better articulate their capabilities, and coming to terms with their job loss reflected in how they presented themselves as confident and capable professionals.

Put aside notions of specially bound leather journals, cloying candles, and precious pens with big plumage floating from the ends. That's not what this is about. It's about a pen (any pen will do), a notebook (go to your drugstore's school supply section and just get one), and the commitment to sitting in place for 30 minutes each day—preferably the same 30 minutes, preferably in the morning, preferably in the same chair.

Sit down and start writing about what is most on your mind. If you're not sure what that is, just start writing. You might start out complaining about the rising cost of cucumbers, but pretty soon your mind will be willing to cooperate and you will find yourself elaborating on your lingering feelings about your last job, your worries about finding a new job, and how you'll continue to make a living.

Write about those things in your work that you particularly enjoy, were most satisfied about in the past (and would like to do again in the future). Write about the people you worked with, particularly their characteristics and how they approached their own work. Write about the challenges you faced, what you learned from them, and what you learned about yourself as you met those challenges. How did success make you feel? How did, perhaps, failure at some challenges make you feel?

Sometimes journaling will be wildly random. Sometimes upsetting or sad. The feeling will go away in a couple hours; if it doesn't, just change the subject and write about something else. Eventually, your focus will turn to those activities (job related or not) that give you a great deal of pleasure in your life. Discount nothing just because you can't seem to immediately connect ways to somehow make a living through those activities. For every passion, hobby, sport, or pastime out there, there are multiple industries designed to support it (or at least capitalize from its popularity). This is a great time to start investigating what those industries might be.

At the same time, don't just stop with the passion itself. You may discover that indulging in the fantasy of opening a bike shop just results in being chained to the store and never getting out on a bike ride yourself. Same with, say, golf, which some describe as a good walk spoiled. Try to get into the business of golf because you love the game so much and you may discover that you've just spoiled for yourself a cherished activity that really does help you get away from work-related cares and concerns. Fun is supposed to be a refuge from work, and maybe it should be honored as such.

But, if you are especially passionate about your pastime, to the point where it's a big part of who you are, explore that in your journal. You may find that the same skills, talents, and abilities that you use in your hobby are also valuable to you in your job.

While you're journaling, ask yourself what it is about the hobby that you love so much. What aspects of your personality or abilities does that favorite activity speak to? Focus (golf)? Discipline (ballet)? Combining patience, tolerance for uncertainty, along with specific knowledge of the object of your ambition (fishing)? The ability to assemble and lead tightly focused teams of strangers (pick-up basketball)? The fun of reacting to rapidly changing environmental conditions and then harnessing them to help you achieve your objective (sailing)?

Do what you love and you'll probably do it well (except for, perhaps, the ballerina idea). At the very least, you'll enjoy the hours and years you devote to improving your abilities, particularly when you understand how to translate those skills, aptitudes, and fascinations into qualities that make you as great at your work as you are in your play. And you'll be able to bring that 20% advantage into the HJM research conversations.

The best thing you can do:
When you write in your journal, really let it rip.

The worst thing you can do:
Keep the feelings you have and the best of who you are bottled up, tamped down, and under wraps.

The first thing you should do:
Plan the time, sit down, and start writing.

Midnight Insight

When the bank where Sarah built her career was bought, she was out of a job. Sarah was the only person among her old neighborhood friends to go to college. She earned more than her father (wherever he is now) and her mother combined. Known to be confident and competent, she had learned a lot about business and finance and could certainly hold her own in the corporate world.

Yet tonight, she felt lost and restless. She turned on her computer, opened a new file, and wrote, "What now?" She stared at the screen for ten minutes. Then she wrote, "My Story."

For three hours straight, often through teary eyes, she wrote the story of how she was raised in a hard and rough neighborhood. As a teenager, she became involved at a local YMCA youth center. She described one counselor at the center who had encouraged her to go to college. "It's clear you have a head on your shoulders. Use it," he used to say.

She described her journey, what she liked in her work and what she didn't like. She realized that she truly enjoyed her volunteer work on the nonprofit boards. She realized that, as a manager, she used the same skills as her YMCA counselor did—encouraging people to do their best and stretch themselves to new challenges. She also thought that many nonprofits needed more business and financial savvy.

After three hours, she went back to the beginning of her document. Under "What now?" she wrote, "Executive director of a nonprofit working with youth." Now focused and freshly inspired, she launched her search. Four months later, she found her job.

CHAPTER 7

Think Like a Hiring Manager

So you do all this work discovering new companies, new possibilities, and openings for a great job—one that will set you squarely on the right path to a new, fulfilling career. Then you go to the interview and everything is going swimmingly. The interviewer, preferably the person you would actually be working for, is extremely excited to meet you. The two of you are clicking; there's real chemistry there, both of you can feel it. Your skillsets are an exact match to the company's need. The air is pulsating with the real potential of a job offer. Your interviewer opens her mouth to speak:

"So what is it about this company (or work or job) that's appealing to you?"

Your answer is straight from the heart: You rhapsodize about how it represents the culmination of all your dreams. You can now see how every job you had up to this point was preparation for this opportunity the two of you are now talking about. This opportunity represents everything to you that you've been looking for, for so, so long. You're fluent in your passion. You're articulate like you've never been before, and you cap it off by talking about the cool offices and great benefits. You don't mind showing your excitement because you know the interviewer gets it.

And you've just blown it.

Searching for the kinds of jobs that would perfectly suit your abilities, motivations, and fit? That's all about you. Attracting multiple job offers from companies with those kinds of jobs? That's not about you at all. That's about the desire, hopes, dreams, and fears of the hiring managers. The sooner you understand the difference, the sooner those great offers will start rolling in.

Because you are reading this book, we consider you our client. So we care about what's on your mind: What will be the job that most satisfyingly speaks to everything you want out of your working hours? How much will it pay? What are the benefits? Will the company be good to work for? How secure will the job be? What would be your next step on the career path? How can you find a dream job in even a hostile economy? Those things are important to us because they're important to you.

But those aren't the considerations that will get you the job offer. What will start generating job offers is the way you understand what's on the mind of the person who might become your boss. And those considerations might have absolutely nothing to do with you.

You still have to understand what those concerns are, though. This is especially essential because you're about to enter an entirely unfamiliar territory. The more you're able to see the industry—and even a potential job—through the eyes of the person who might hire you, the more you'll be able to speak about the opportunities and needs from the perspective of your "buyer." And ultimately, the faster you'll begin to attract job offers.

Successful salespeople will tell you that the trick to moving products and services is to find out what's keeping the customer up at night and speak directly to those concerns. That's a much better approach than to constantly pitch the details on your resumé and the benefits you bring to the table. Your potential hiring managers are your "customers," and your job is to understand how *they* think, what *they* worry about, how *they* behave, and how *they* make their buying (in this case, hiring) decisions. Not how passionate you are about the position.

Here are just a few concerns that might be rocketing around in their heads while they're speaking with you about your own career journey and how it might intersect with their needs:

"I know I need help, I just don't know what kind of help I need."

"Ugh, how many times do I have to fill this position until I get it right? Could this person be just another embarrassing experiment?"

"It sure would be nice to find the person who will help me please my boss more effectively."

"I've had the job this person wants; no one can do it as well as I can."

"I've never even done that job, how can I know if this person can do a job that I don't understand myself?"

"The company is moving in an entirely different direction; this new hire must bring something completely new to the table. I only wish I knew what it was."

"This industry isn't what it once was. Maybe I should hire this outsider to give us some fresh perspective."

"How can I even hope to find someone who meets not only my criteria, but the conflicting needs of the various departments that we work with?"

"How can I hope to find someone who meets my exacting standards for excellence?"

Some of these concerns will be shared by managers throughout the industry or profession you're exploring. Some will be specific to the individual managers themselves. In either case, when you use the HJM research meetings to dig below the surface, you'll come away with the essential insights that will give you the competitive advantage when the time comes to actually go after a specific job possibility.

When you're using the HJM research techniques, you are in control of the meeting, so you get to ask the questions (at least a lot more of them than you would in a traditional job interview, where all you are initially is just the human representation of your resumé). So use your questions to better understand how your prospective hiring managers see the world, what they value and what they worry about:

"Tell me about the best people you hired for this job. What were the qualities that made them a success? Are those qualities still relevant in today's environment?"

"Tell me about a hire who didn't work out, especially in this kind of role. If it was an issue of fit, how would you describe the disconnect?"

"How has your business changed in recent years, especially as the economy turned?"

"What keeps you excited about the work you do?"

"If you could add one thing to the mix of skills in your staff, what would it be? What would you subtract?"

"What do people in this industry find funny? Is there a joke that's making the rounds?" (Be prepared to laugh politely. And remember the joke; you might be able to use it as an icebreaker in later HJM research meetings.)

"How have performance issues or standards for excellence changed in recent years? What's essential for the future?"

"What must be in place for the departments to work well together? What are the challenges there?"

The answers to these questions are important enough, to be sure. But the real value comes in what you actually do with these answers in subsequent HJM research meetings. Keep in mind that each one of these meetings is not an official job interview, but a knowledge-, understanding- and insight-gathering mission. As you start seeing patterns with the accumulated information from all these HJM research meetings, you will start understanding what's important to the people you will be encountering on your new career path and what's not. You'll be able to identify what gaps in your own abilities and experiences you might need to start closing.

And then when you are in meetings that you actually want to move toward being actual job interviews, you can transform that accumulated understanding into strategically worded questions designed to help you reveal what you bring to the table. That said, you must first demonstrate that you see the world through your hiring manager's eyes.

"Many people I've spoken with have told me that success in this profession requires these kinds of qualities: _____. Do you think that's true? Would you have anything else to add to that list? Really? Well, let me tell you what I've done along those lines.... Because I would really like to talk to you about taking a job in this field."

This is when magic happens. You are able to talk about your abilities and motivations in terms that your potential boss will understand, because clearly you understand your potential boss's worries and challenges. You've already demonstrated that through your knowledgeable observations and thoughtful analysis. And your prospective boss will think, "Wow, this person really gets it."

"How soon can you start?"

The best thing you can do:
In every meeting, every networking connection, use it as an opportunity to learn more about your target profession, even if you think you know it all.

The worst thing you can do:
Hard sell yourself.

The first thing you should do:
Keep in mind that it's always the buyer who will make the ultimate purchasing decision. In your case, your buyer is the hiring manager.

Corporate Translations

After he got out of the Navy, Paul was frustrated because he couldn't get a job. Not only could he not get a job, he couldn't even get an interview. People certainly respected his accomplishment in qualifying as an elite Navy SEAL. They just didn't know what to do with someone who knew how to wear black face paint, land on sandy beaches, and blow things up. Encouraged by his career coach, Paul started interviewing managers about what they thought was important in top-quality employees. What was the best hire they ever made? And the worst? He asked about the difference between an average employee and the top 10% performer. Finally, he asked about what came to mind when they thought about the training and experience of a Navy SEAL. From their answers, he was able to piece together an understanding of the biases people would have when they met him. He also began to highlight the training and experience that make a Navy SEAL a great employee. But he did so using the language a business manager—not a commando—would understand.

STEP 2

CONNECT YOUR HOTTEST SKILLS TO WHAT HIRING MANAGERS REALLY CARE ABOUT

CHAPTER 8

Ability, Motivation, Fit: The Top Three Factors for the Ideal Job

No question. The traditional job search method (if you could call it that) is easy. It just doesn't work that well. You find an announcement of an opening that remotely matches what you've done before. You apply. And then you wait. After you get desperate enough, you broaden your search criteria to include jobs you have no interest in at all, that have nothing to do with your background, and that may require that you compete with teenagers for summer minimum wage. See how easy that is? After a while, you become so accustomed to turning a deaf ear to what really ignites your interests. And pretty soon, you forget those job specifications that would completely engage you. Which is probably a good thing, because the more you're willing to compromise for the sake of landing a paying gig, the further away you move from that realm of the *ideal job*. In the forgetting, you may not feel the pain so much.

The hidden job market (HJM), on the other hand, demands much more participation from you, with the reward being a greater likelihood that you will find the ideal job. The problem is that, by this time, you might have forgotten what that is. Good pay and benefits are a good start—especially when you're feeling the pinch of the financial emergency. But once those basic, security-related needs are met, you will hunger for a job that meets less-tangible requirements. Because you're taking on the extra work of the hidden job market anyway, why not use this extra effort to land the ideal job right now, so at the very least, you'll be happily ensconced in work that truly speaks to you and your needs?

The trouble is this: Maybe you've forgotten what elements make up the ideal job. If you've been busy chasing after those publicly announced jobs, who can blame you if you need a little refresher on the three critical factors that make the job ideal for you. Taken one at a time, each nets you a so-so opportunity. But lace the three together, and you've got a solid picture of the job qualities that will reward you with so much more than just a paycheck and halfway tolerable benefits.

Ability

The first critical success factor might seem to be the most straightforward at first. This is the category that is the most frequently seen on a resumé, because it has to do with your knowledge, technical understanding, tools (business and technical), management skills, trainings, certifications, and so forth. And that's a good start. But the real question is this: Sure, you have these abilities that you can list on your resumé, but how many of these abilities do you want to continue using in your career?

To uncover those abilities (maybe even discover some that you might have overlooked in the dreariness of recent years when you were slightly off-course in your career), make a list of 12 to 15 events in your professional life (recent grads: think school, volunteering, and internships) that you consider to be true accomplishments. These aren't degrees or skills, these are stories of times when you used your skills, education, or even innate talents to make a difference in your work or business.

- What challenge or opportunity were you presented with?
- What abilities did you call on to achieve success in that situation?

- What was *success* in that challenge? This could be anything from cost savings to revenue generation, to customer retention, to expanding the potential of your organization. In other words, what was the business benefit of that success?
- What did you learn about yourself in the process? What a-ha moment emerged from this success that broadened your ideas about what you might be capable of?

You might think that a list of 12 to 15 accomplishments is somewhat excessive (especially if you can't even think of that many actual skills that you can claim). But remember that these are scenarios when you used your abilities to achieve a positive outcome for your company. And the purpose is not only to reacquaint yourself with a list of the wide range of things you can do, but to get you to think about how many of those things you really want to continue to do.

Which leads us to....

Motivation

You have an ability. And some company is willing to pay you for it. That doesn't mean that you're stuck on that career path forever. If some ability doesn't leave you feeling deeply satisfied, why shackle yourself to it for the rest of your working life?

This is not to say that you have to jettison the ability altogether. Maybe a slight tweak or alteration will transform a particular ability from leaden handcuffs to a true gift that will put your career back on the right track.

For instance, one of Duncan's clients was in human resources. She had spent the previous two years downsizing and restructuring her company. So, she was very skilled and experienced in identifying jobs that were expendable. When the time came for her to review her own career, she knew one thing for absolutely sure: She didn't want to be in the business of firing people anymore. Even though that was an accomplishment that benefitted an organizational objective, she needed to give herself permission to exclude those abilities that she was good at but that drained her soul.

Duncan was able to show her that she could take that same skill, do it in a slightly (or significantly) different way, and reframe her ability to do something that motivated her. When considering her recent experience identifying which employees to lay off, she realized that she had also been identifying talent *to keep*. So, after she was able to see the light side of the dark coin, she could then effectively (and truthfully) tell the story of how she helped her CEO build future bench strength in her company by identifying the top high-potential, high-performing, essential talent in a smaller organization.

It's not enough to be able to do a job; you really deserve a job that you *want* to do. If you're not interested in the work, if it breaks your heart, if it separates you from your values or even morals, now is a really good time to realize that. And use this hidden job market project as your chance to stop punishing yourself with work that leaves you cold inside. And find work that really motivates you.

Your motivation can come in a variety of forms. Perhaps you enjoy being in a position where you can influence major decisions, for instance. Or you have the opportunity to be of service to others in a significant way. Or you can exercise your creativity on the job. Or you enjoy the energy of being in an entrepreneurial role.

When you look at your list of accomplishments, you'll begin to see hints of what makes you feel emotionally engaged in your jobs.

That's motivation. Write those elements down.

Fit

The issue of fit can be broken down into two fundamental areas: who you do your job with and where do you do it, which is about the actual environment.

Environment: Are you happy to work inside office buildings? Do you need the noise and hustle-bustle of factory floors? Do you prefer to spend your days away from the office, taking full advantage of the technology of virtual offices? Do you prefer an edgy, happening corporate culture where just about any behavior is tolerated, so long as it doesn't end up in citations and court costs? Or are you most comfortable in a buttoned-down culture, where rules of behavior are sharply defined? Can you tolerate working in a bullpen of cubicles? Or would you rather be outdoors at a job site happily tapping away on your laptop?

And what about the people you actually work with? Every job has various levels of stakeholders who work with you: your boss, your coworkers, your customers, even your subordinates. What kind of overall working culture makes you happy? A collegial, egalitarian one in which everyone has a stake and a say in your product or service? A strictly enforced hierarchical one in which there is clarity as to who answers to whom all the way up and down the organizational food chain (we mean, org chart)? Are you happiest and most productive in a culture of trust and autonomy? Or do you prefer a system where all action items, deliverables, and goals are micromeasured in a drive for results?

AMF: Putting It Together

At first glance, discovering your *abilities, motivation,* and *fit* (AMF) may appear to be a simplistic exercise of self-discovery. Perhaps a familiar version of many self-discovery exercises that you've undertake over the years. That's okay. Do it anyway. If you have managed your career in recent years using the career search technique of take-what-you-get published job listings, you may have lost yourself somewhere along the way, forfeiting the job you want for the job that's been offered to you. And you might have forgotten what really does make you feel completely engaged in that sweet spot of *just the right job, for just the right company, with just the right people.*

If you go through all the effort that plumbing the hidden job market requires, don't you at least owe it to yourself to reach for the absolute best possibility that is waiting for you to discover?

Knowing what your AMF is will help you get the best from this entire process, giving you the courage to say "no thanks" to the job offers that are almost-but-not-quite-right. And the confidence that when you do discover that job opportunity that's absolutely perfect for you, you'll know yourself well enough to say yes.

The best thing you can do:
Give yourself permission to let go of the skills and abilities you have that you dread or simply leave you cold.

The worst thing you can do:
Give into temptation and say yes to the wrong job. You won't be available to say yes to the right job when it finally comes along.

The first thing you should do:
Put yourself through the AMF exercise and hold on tight to the results as the essential guidelines that will govern whether you say yes to a job.

They Kept Promoting Him, But He Hated Being a VP

Ed loved all things automotive, and he worked for a company that published information for the car business. Because his passion made him so good at his job, he was constantly promoted—to the level of vice president, where he was no longer doing what he loved. He was managing other people who did what he loved. And he didn't love managing people. When he sat down and wrote out his contributions he was most proud of, being a boss didn't appear on the list. But he did list innovation, creating business partnerships, doing deals, and using his deep knowledge of the automotive marketplace. He also realized he preferred working with the leadership of smaller companies over the larger corporations. His understanding of abilities, motivations, and fit (AMF) gave him new enthusiasm and focus in his search. Skip the vice president title, he resolved, and in his new career, he made more money without the headaches.

CHAPTER 9

Maybe You Were Fired for Fit, Not Failure: Recovery from a Job Disaster

If you were fired or laid off from your last job—a job that you had thrown all your passion and energies into—it could have been because you did all the right things. It was just for the wrong people. It could have been an overuse of a strength, or a style, that got you into trouble; only the people who fired you made sure you would believe you screwed up.

Martha, for instance, loves to tell the story of how she got fired from a bookstore. Just to put things into perspective for you, Martha doesn't just love to write books, she loves books. Period. (As most writers do, of course.) Put her in a house with cats (three's her limit), towers of books, and provide sustenance of coffee, chocolate, and music, and she's good. For weeks. Amazon.com must have had her in mind when it invented the one-click convenience. But, when it comes to the commerce of books, she mostly loves bookstores. That clean, fresh smell of brand new paper and ink (not to mention the enchanting cover designs) does something to her brain. It makes her buy more books, is what it does.

So it would follow that asking her to sell books would be natural, wouldn't it? One summer, while doing a writerly sojourn on Cape Cod, she decided to take a part-time job at the local village bookstore. She lasted three weeks. The problem wasn't immediately apparent. She upsold happy customers regularly, turning their single paperback purchase into a shopping bag filled with hardbacks. She even sold them books that the tiny store didn't have in stock, promising to arrange a special order for them and ship the books back to their homes. That cash register sang. She was fired. Why? All those multiple special orders caused the owner to stay late every night, resentfully doing the paperwork and missing her dinner. Martha's exuberance overwhelmed the tiny store. Passion for the product netted her the pink slip. For Martha, to get fired from a bookstore was a low point. (But she can laugh about it now.)

Feel better? It happens all the time in the business world, from little, charming shops in little charming Cape Cod villages to multinational corporations. When we invest our gifts and passions in an organization that doesn't want it, need it, or care about it, we run the risk of derailing ourselves and our careers.

In Duncan's work as an executive coach, he has often been asked to work with people who were fired from their jobs. They feel as though their careers are in shambles because the last thing they heard about their place in the work world was that they had no value as an employee. Indeed, if they were treated unkindly in the termination conversation, they could even pick up the message that, as far as employers are concerned, their very presence inside the building could actually be a liability. And that just doesn't make for a confident job seeker who is asking for Duncan's help.

While working with these clients—truly hard-working people who deserved to find a good job—Duncan began to see some patterns emerge. They all began to point to the fact that the very reason they were let go from the last job could be the very thing that could attract their next employer. This principle applies to you, too. Here's how:

What you did well was not important to your employer, and you tended to neglect the rest of your job. Often, people are more interested in doing the things they do well—at the expense of those tasks that they don't do well or aren't interested in. So they put those things off, don't do them well, can't do them at all, or exude an ambivalent attitude when they finally settle down to the humdrum. Naturally, that becomes a source of dissatisfaction with their boss. If you identify with this scenario, take advantage of the fact that the hidden job market (HJM) will give you the chance at a better match or to even participate in writing your own job description. And seek out those opportunities that don't require you to do those tasks (or at least give you the budget or ability to delegate those tasks to other people).

A great way to separate those job characteristics and tasks you love from those you don't is to review the jobs you have had. In one column, write down those aspects of the jobs you found to be satisfying. In a second column, write down those aspects that did not meet your abilities, motivation, or fit. Here is what you might discover:

- Those things you did well and were valued by your employer were the most satisfying.
- Those things you did well that the employer did not care about were sources of your frustration.
- Those things you did not do well that were valued by your employer were points of friction.

(What you did well, you might have overdone. This is probably where Martha comes in with her bookstore story. Every strength has a downside when overdone. As a result, you come off looking like a weak performer. The solution here is to perhaps tone down your passion a bit—so that when your next employer, who truly does want you precisely for that strength, will appreciate it when it's delivered in more measured, considered doses.)

Or find a corporate culture that celebrates your over-the-top passion and talents for your job. And have a ball.

Whatever you do, don't accept the assumption that the very thing that gives you joy is the very thing that gets you fired. And that somehow it's your fault and failing. It's not you. It's not even your employer. It's just a bad match.

But if you've been repeatedly criticized by people—well meaning or not—for being who you are, there are two approaches to take. One is to find a better fit where you can reframe or describe your weakness as a strength for the right employer. The second approach is to develop new skills to take the edge off your overused strengths. This can take some thought (another good use for your journal, by the way). The following table might help you reframe your weaknesses as strengths and help you define the right employers who will hire you precisely because you are who you are.

Your Weakness Has Been Described As	Organizations May Want to Hire You Because Your Strength Is	Keep Your Overused Strength from Hurting You By
Ready-fire-aim mentality.	Your flexibility to adjust to changing conditions.	Setting aside some time to plan. Learn that involving others may keep your objectives from being derailed.
Inflexible, overdependent on rules, regulations, and procedures.	Your ability to plan and execute to plan, ensure consistent policies are applied, and create order out of chaos.	Thinking about how to help people navigate complex rules to achieve the needs of the business. Use humor and empathy
Too emotional.	Your deep commitment to team and business success and your sensitivity to client and customer needs.	Knowing when you are getting in too deep and need to step back. Never send email when feeling agitated. Save it and review it later.

Your Weakness Has Been Described As	Organizations May Want to Hire You Because Your Strength Is	Keep Your Overused Strength from Hurting You By
Prefer to immerse yourself in the technical competence over social graces.	Your commitment to being a reliable resource for essential information, and your passion for the right answer.	Learning more about other people's objectives and what they are trying to accomplish. Offer help. Gain perspective of a bigger picture.
Inattentive to administrative detail—poor administrator.	Your ability to focus on urgent priorities and to get the most out of the day.	Preventing paperwork from piling up to the point that catching up is a huge project. Schedule time for it. Think about how good it will feel to get it off your back. Or maybe you could find someone else to do it. Find somebody who does it well to teach you her technique/system.
Political missteps.	Your ability to see issues for what they are, the fact that you are nonpolitical and can be counted on for honest assessment, and your ability to stand alone and operate in the field.	Finding a mentor. Gain perspective of each player and what their job goals are; what is their measure of success by their stakeholders?
Failure to hit goals.	Your willingness to do root cause analysis of performance challenges, learn from mistakes, and better align goals with both capabilities and interests.	Learning to negotiate unreasonable goals or resources to achieve the goals. Take jobs that have goals that engage you.

Your Weakness Has Been Described As	Organizations May Want to Hire You Because Your Strength Is	Keep Your Overused Strength from Hurting You By
Micromanagement.	Your attention to detail and results, and the fact that you are unwilling to accept average performance that causes mediocre results.	Learning the art of delegation. Improve your ability to pick people.
Arrogant/results at all costs.	Your high personal performance standards for self and others, and the fact that you need to be surrounded by the best and that you work best when presented with difficult intellectual challenges, can work around obstacles, and often exceeds goals.	Understanding it all comes back to haunt you eventually. You may be tempted to break or bend rules, as well as run roughshod over others, for short-term results. The best go furthest when grounded in integrity, values, and ethics. Learn to tolerate other people's work styles and inspire the best of those you think are "B" players.
Workaholic.	Your energy and stamina, particularly when faced with big challenges.	Scheduling time for other challenges— adventure, learning, play. Use your downtime to get regain balance.

The best thing you can do:
Keep in mind that your strengths can be detrimental to your career if you find yourself in the wrong job with the wrong company.

The worst thing you can do:
Ignore behavior problems (this includes substance-abuse issues) that are impacting your work, as well as your personal life. Get help.

The first thing you should do:
Consider the table and see how you might be able to translate possible criticisms into advantages.

The Root Cause of a Culture Misfit

While working for a large corporation, Sam earned his black belt in Six Sigma. Despite his highly respected expertise in problem solving, he lost his job when the corporation went through a restructuring. So Sam took his black belt credentials and hit the job market.

In his networking, he met the CEO of a small company—a man who saw the value of Six Sigma as a tool for helping his organization move beyond some of its systemic problems and realize its potential. So Sam and the CEO wholeheartedly struck a deal, and Sam happily went to work for this smaller company, giving it the benefit of all the sophisticated knowledge and tools he picked up at his previous employer.

One problem: The second-level executives hated the changes that Sam was recommending. They were too busy being caught up in the day-to-day emergencies and workload to stop and reconsider systemic changes. But they couldn't reject the CEO's pet project of bringing Six Sigma into the organization. And so, human nature being what it is, they turned against Sam himself. After the CEO heard enough complaints about how insufferable Sam was as a coworker, he fired him.

Again, human nature being what it is, Sam took it personally. And why not? The complaints were personal. And the termination was certainly personal. But what was the root cause of the actual problem? Bad breath? No. Bad timing. The CEO and his company simply weren't ready for the discipline required of implementing Six Sigma into the company culture. (They don't call it "black belt" for nothing.)

Now it was up to Sam to figure out how to explain his job loss and avoid making that career mistake again. He decided to prequalify the readiness of any company (and its leadership) that expresses interest in Six Sigma: "Although senior executives and CEOs may believe that Six Sigma is what they want, they really have to understand that it takes a lot of time and effort to properly implement it into their culture. In my last company, I realized they were not really ready to make that investment despite what Six Sigma could do for their company. Based on that experience, I can help you figure out if you're ready for it or not. If you're not sure that you are ready for the change, I'm probably not the right person for you and I would recommend you continue what you are doing now."

As a result of this analysis, by the time he negotiated his next serious job offer, he was able to specify exactly what cultural factors needed to be in place to ensure success. Because he was willing to walk away from a culture misfit, he gave himself his best chance of finding the cultural fit that made him successful the next time around.

CHAPTER 10

Don't Have the Exact Experience? No Problem!

Despite the many generations of humanity participating in job interviews (people looking for jobs and people hoping to hire the ideal candidate), the process is still riddled with so much dysfunction. You know it; we know it; and they (the corporate monolithic *they* who seem to be in control of everything—but they're not) know it. The most pernicious of all the dysfunctions, it seems, is the simple fact that *they* want someone with proven experience in doing exactly the same job in the same industry (three years' experience seems to be ideal).

But this book isn't about them. It's about *you*. And you want to get on with things and actually grow yourself and your career by doing something more than what you've been doing the last three years. You might want to be doing something really different than before. Or maybe you do want to do the same thing but in a different industry. Even if you're only hoping to make small, incremental changes, there's going to be a credibility/competency gap between what you did last and what you want to be doing next.

The trick is this: convincing your target companies that you're actually up to the challenge of taking on a whole new set of responsibilities in a whole new environment, maybe even industry or profession. Of course, you already know that you are perfectly capable of taking on new and different job responsibilities. You have done it many times during your career, right? You are smart, and you learn fast. You know it. Now, you just have to make sure your hiring manager knows it. You remember this from Chapter 7, "Think Like a Hiring Manager": It is all about seeing your abilities through the hiring manager's eyes. This chapter gives you the tools to do exactly that.

Assuming you know what kind of job you want, you may also have some idea about what skills, background, previous experiences, and other qualifications your targeted job might require. You've probably noticed already that there are gaps in your background that you believe might keep you from the kind of job you want. At this point, even the smallest changes may feel so overwhelming that you're tempted to just give up this crazy notion of recalibrating your career. Maybe you have already spoken with a couple of people, or perhaps you have seen some ads for the kind of job you want, but their stated minimum requirements don't match your background at all. Or maybe you have already been rejected for a position because of some weird fit issue. ("Although you are an accountant, our industry's accounting is completely different from accounting in the industry you worked in before. It just won't be a fit.")

You know you can do the job. But those gaps feel like an early-warning system that you could be setting yourself up for rejection. They're not. They just indicate what gaps need to be closed.

Very few jobs stand on the other edge of a competency or capability gap so big that it's impossible (for you) to close. You just need a strategy to manage those gaps. (In fact, if there are no gaps, it's possible that you've set your own ambition for change and growth too low. If you're committed to the hidden job market (HJM) process, at least be sure that you'll be rewarded with a fantastic new career as an outcome.) Again, the beauty of the HJM research meetings is that you get an advance look at all the different requirements of your target job *before* you actually start formally interviewing for one.

But first, you have to do just a little advance work. This way, as you start going to HJM research meetings—and especially as they begin to morph into full-on job interviews—you'll be completely prepared to close those gaps in your meeting partner's mind. Here's how:

Take a piece of paper and make two columns. In the left column, list AMF elements from your background. Be specific (and calm; don't let the energy of negative self-talk drive you into the kitchen... this is a listing exercise, not a judging exercise). Those items for the left column include your abilities (your knowledge, skills, and accomplishments), all the things that motivate you in your work, and what your criteria is for a good fit.

In the right column, list the essential criteria for your target job *from the hiring manager's perspective*. This includes both objective qualifications for the job (knowledge, skills, experience) and what the hiring manager perceives (considering the company's culture or industry personality) to be the right motivators and personality that might create the right "fit." Then, there's that top 20% factor. We're not talking about the minimum requirements for the position. We're talking about those qualities that truly set a person apart. (As you conduct HJM research meetings, you'll ask your meeting partners what makes a person especially successful in this culture. The answers to that question make up the top 20% factor.)

Then, compare the two lists. You'll start seeing gaps between what you bring to the table and what your potential hiring manager is looking for. Good. That's what we want you to see at this point. Now, you can start organizing them and strategizing how to deal with them—*before* being caught tongue-tied in the all-critical job interview.

Gap conditions fall into four categories:

1. **No gap.** Your background fits their needs perfectly in every way. Great! You will want to test these further to make sure that your meeting partners see the connection as well as you do. So far, so good.

    Fix. None needed.

2. **Real gap.** You need education, certification, or a license to do the job. You aren't there yet, and you are unlikely to be seriously considered for a job you might want because of that gap.

    Fix. Unless we're talking rocket science or brain surgery (and if you weren't a rocket scientist or brain surgeon before), very few job categories won't accommodate a mid-career change—assuming you're really motivated to do the work to prepare yourself. You can take direct action to start closing that gap. Start the licensure process now. Enroll in the certification training course, start taking classes toward the degree that hiring managers typically request for this position.*

    Even though this might seem like a hassle for a possible pie-in-the-sky notion, there are immediate advantages to taking action to close this gap now. First, you demonstrate your motivation to hiring managers—that you are so committed to preparing yourself for this work that you've initiated the training process yourself. Second, this kind of training for

---

*Take extension courses throughout your career (as a matter of fact, even when you're not actively searching for a new job). Not only are you keeping up with your career, but you are positioning yourself within a goldmine of networking contacts. The teachers of these courses are often leaders in their profession or industry. And your classmates will be your potential peers.

your new field will give you the chance to determine whether this is really something you want to do. It's a chance to try it on, even in the context of a classroom simulation. If you discover that the training is a snore, that's a valuable sneak preview for how you might actually not enjoy the work itself.

Alternatively, look for a company that doesn't require the certification or formal education before it will give you a chance at the job. Many professions have associations that provide a certification process that measures your command of the body of knowledge core to the work. And some companies get into the habit of insisting that job candidates have that certification. But, unlike licensure, certification is not a legal requirement. So, find the company that's not asking for the certification. Get your start there.

3.   **Perception gap.** You did the same thing in your previous career, but they call it something else. You clearly see the connection between what you did in the past and what you want to do in the future. But, the people you talk to during your HJM meetings aren't getting it. And if they're not getting it, you know that hiring managers won't get it either. That's the perception gap.

Fix. Use your HJM meetings to discover clues into how to close that gap. Learn how to talk about your experience in the language that hiring managers understand. What are the terms of the trade? The industry jargon? The common acronyms? Even the jokes that reveal certain attitudes prevalent in the profession? Ask your HJM meeting partners to describe a situation in your target job area that went really well. Ask what essential qualities made that circumstance successful? What typically happens when something goes wrong? Understanding in detail the world of your target job, including the challenges, successes, and even potential pitfalls, will give you essential clues into how your skills and abilities fit with the job.

Then, when you're in formal job interviews, use that insight (and your new vocabulary) to frame your own stories. This way, your background speaks directly to the hiring manager concerns, in their language.

4. **Negative bias gap.** This is an opinion that someone has against you based on stereotype. Age and race prejudices quickly come to mind as examples. And those kinds of biases are especially insidious because hiring managers who cling to those ideas are also practiced in hiding them (usually).

But, negative biases can also extend to your work experience, such as what you did, what industry you were in, or what companies you worked for. Maybe you're coming from a dying industry, so hiring managers might perceive you to be old-fashioned or a player in a failure. Or you could be coming from a sector that's currently out of favor in general public opinion. Or people can't quite see how someone with your industry background could possibly be a match with their industry needs. (How, for instance, could someone who has worked in a highly regulated, process-driven industry possibly perform in a creative start-up that depends on creative customer service as a distinguishing factor?)

Even positive bias could work against you. Duncan says that there is one company in San Diego, where he lives, that is always held up as the company to work for because of its popular product and famous corporate culture. So what could possibly be wrong with *you* if you want to leave that company and work anywhere else? Obviously, you must have a screw loose.

Fix. Think of the things that you worry most about that could come up in the job interview and have a strategy to address those biases in advance. If you are thinking, "Gosh, I hope they don't ask me about *that*," get your responses to *that* ready now. Here are some strategies for addressing negative biases:

- **Completely agree with the hiring manager, but then distance yourself from the questionable characteristic.** This works well when you're being asked about an industry or profession change. "I know exactly how you feel. I've come to the same conclusion. That industry was missing some very important qualities to keep it relevant and meaningful."

- **Acknowledge the bias.** Use the salesperson's technique of *feel, felt, found*. "I know exactly how you *feel*. A lot of people have *felt* the same way about my background (the company, the profession, the culture). In fact, I once felt that way, too. But, what they (old bosses, customers, coworkers) *found* about me was that there really is a natural fit between what I do and how I do it and what your company needs now."

- **Show how the characteristic that makes you questionable as a fit could be a competitive advantage for the new company.** The quality that makes you "different" could be the key to opening up a new market for the organization, for instance. Your background of doing work entirely unrelated to your target company's critical objectives could give your new employer just the kind of fresh, outsider insight that they need for breakthrough thinking.

Finally, the key to really closing the important gaps is your ability to talk about what puts you in that 20% category of high-performing employees. Once you get the biases and barriers out of the way (even if they're only in your mind), drive the conversation to lift you out of the "minimum qualifications" arena and into the group that exhibits excellence. The differences between your background and what a potential employer is looking for could actually be the source of the 20% edge that the hiring manager wants.

In other words: You may be just what they're looking for. Only they don't know it yet. Now you have the tools to tell them.

The best thing you can do:
If you want to break into a new career or industry, focus much of your HJM research meetings on finding people who have already done so (preferably people with your background).

The worst thing you can do:
Allow people to discourage you because you don't have the background that is an exact match to the traditional hiring requirements.

The first thing you should do:
Ask the vice president of membership for your local industry trade group (who is in a great position to know almost everyone who is successful in your targeted field) for an introduction to someone who does the kind of job you want.

From Banking to Social Work

Sarah was an executive vice president at a bank, but she loved volunteer work. Having grown up in a disadvantaged community herself, she credited a caring social worker for helping her get an early successful start in life. And now, she was committed to giving back in a significant way.

Among other activities, she sat on boards of directors for nonprofit social service and arts organizations. As a board member, she noticed many nonprofits weren't very sophisticated in financial management or in how they solicited corporate support. She also realized that a good executive director could make a decent salary. When she was laid off from her bank job as a result of a merger, she applied for two open director positions in nonprofits. Although interviewers were polite and even agreed that her financial skills would be an asset, she didn't get the job. She lost out to other applicants who had more experience or advanced degrees in social work or public policy.

She knew she could do the job, but realized that she must be missing an essential qualification. So she interviewed several people in nonprofits to learn more about what made someone successful as an executive director, as well as to learn more about the preconceptions nonprofits might have about banking executives. As a result of this additional research she dramatically changed her approach to her search, emphasizing her personal passion for the nonprofits' causes. She told her personal story about growing up in a poor and rough neighborhood.

Second, she borrowed graduate school textbooks from a professor at the local school of social work and learned the terms and policy issues related to community service agencies.

Third, she developed a "feel-felt-found" statement to deal with the prejudice that people might have about bankers. For example, she would say, "When most people think about banking, they think about aloof executives in three-piece suits. When I was growing up, I felt the same way. The reality is, when I was running a neighborhood branch early in my career, I learned the practicalities of dealing with whomever walked in the door. They might be confused, angry, worried, or just looking for help. My greatest joy was being of service and helping my employees, many of whom were just starting their career, learn the skills to be effective with the public. Best of all, I learned how to manage the budget and get the most from every dollar. In fact, I even won an award for the best branch for both service to clients' needs and financial efficiency. Many people in social service agencies have told me those are essential capabilities that make a good executive director a great executive director."

In her next interview, she convinced the board she was the perfect choice for the job over other more experienced non-profit professional administrators.

STEP 3

UPGRADE YOUR NETWORKING TO GET BETTER RESULTS

CHAPTER 11

How to Make Networking Really Work, Really

Networking is on everyone's mind right now. Our friends are talking about the need to do more networking and go to more networking events. Companies are offering workshops and seminars on the subject. Television news anchors are interviewing experts on networking tips. Even as we're writing this chapter, we received a media request for ideas on how to remember peoples' names at networking events. Our advice: Don't bother going to those networking events in the first place. Pure heresy.

Everyone's talking about networking, but almost everyone is still networking badly. It's not about the number of business cards you collect. It's not about standing ever-so-nonchalantly by the buffet salad hoping to meet someone who knows someone (only to find yourself meeting someone *else* who is hoping to meet someone who knows someone). It's not even about making friends, believe it or not. You can go to all the lunches you want to, until you weigh 450 pounds, and bond over news and weather and sports, and it won't get you closer to a job opportunity that you would want. You might get a friend out of the experience, maybe someone to go to Weight Watchers with.

And what about all those friends you have? Surely someone must know of a job out there. This is how it typically goes: You print off copies of your resumé. Then you summon up the right "can do" upbeat sound in your voice, meet your friends for lunch or coffee, and say, "You know of any job?" "Yes, there might be something going on over in such-in-such department." "Wow! This networking thing really works! Here, would you please pass my resumé on to the hiring manager?" And then… wait for it… nothing.

Where did the resumé go? Did it get lost in a pile? Did this mysterious hiring manager ever see it? Did he give it the once over, decide you aren't right for the role, and get on with his day? Did your friend even pass it on? You can't exactly ask your contact because you don't want to put her on the spot. (After all, think back to the last time you were asked to pass on a resumé. What did you do with that thing? You *think* you passed it along. Did you?)

It's said that there are an average of six degrees of separation between us and anyone we want to meet in the world. And that may be true. Research on social networks seems to confirm this and even suggests that the maximum number of degrees might be around twelve. The problem is that you might be five degrees from Warren Buffet, which would make you six degrees from Bill Gates (they are good friends). But even if you would love to work for the Bill and Melinda Gates Foundation, that doesn't mean you will get introduced. As a result, the kind of networking we see out there usually stops at Degree 2—a friend of a friend. Then: dead end.

"Two degrees of separation" networking can be limiting. And once it is played out, it will get you absolutely nowhere. You'll end up with a lot of concerned but burned-out friends who are really tired of hearing about your frustrations of getting a job. They've run out of ideas, and frankly, they may be more reluctant to introduce you to anyone else.

Your business and social relationships are still an important first step of your networking, but you want to get beyond them as effectively as you can. Before you get to the situation where they cross the street when they see you coming, think about how your Degree 1 friends can be enlisted to help you move beyond even their immediate circles and cast you far into the more distant degrees and new circles of experts and potential relationships.

Even though many companies have turned to employee referrals for filling jobs (which is the rare event where your Degree 1 friends can really come in handy), the chances are excellent that you haven't even met the person who will steer you to the person who will ultimately hire you. That person may be seven degrees away from you right this minute. So excellent networking is all about getting to that person—and in such a way that all those people from Degree 1 through Degree 6 are still happy to follow your progress.

Because most job seekers don't network very well, with a little effort, you can move ahead of the pack. These are the key points to remember when you conduct a really great networking campaign that truly works for you:

- **A main objective is to cluster jump.** Social networks tend to form in clusters around common interests, geographies, industries, and expertise. The real treasure most likely lies beyond the borders of your map of currently known contacts. If you just stick with those you know and whom they know, your boundaries will be pretty narrow. Seek out people you don't even know (yet) but who are likely to know the people you want to meet. For instance: membership officers of your local association; professors; subject matter experts (like authors) and consultants in your field. It might be a little uncomfortable to cold call or email these people for the first time. But you'll get over it with practice. It won't be long before you'll be able to reach out to whole new sets of contacts because of a personal introduction from these people you've met. And thus, your network expands into new clusters of associates that you wouldn't have been able to approach through your core relationships.

- **Even though you're looking for your next role, there is so much more value to networking than the simple yes/no question.** Be upfront about the fact that you're looking for your next role, but recognize the value of each networking meeting as the chance to learn something new about your profession, industry, or community. This is an important advantage regardless of your situation, but it's especially crucial if you hope to change professions or even geographic locations. If you just go into these meetings with the sole question on your mind, "Know of any job openings?," your networking partner will quickly say no, even if the truth might be yes.

  Networking isn't just about meeting people. It's about gathering information along the way: information to help you refine your thinking, gain deeper insights, and understand the current issues in the industry (what the current issues and concerns are that could be so cutting-edge that they haven't even been written about in the industry press yet).

- **It's important to conduct your networking campaign in such a way that people will continue to care about you long after you have left.** No matter how far flung into the frontier of degrees you are conducting your networking meetings, chances are that no single meeting will immediately generate a job lead. That's disappointing, sure. But it's really okay. Those opportunities could be right around the corner. And the greater the number of people who are looking out for you, the better the chances that someone will call or email you with juicy news. Duncan tells his clients that it is a sign of success when they hear about the same job opening through multiple sources. That means, he says, that you've created a solidly constructed network of people who truly care about what happens to you next. And these people may not even know each other.

How do you get total strangers to care about you and your job search? It boils down to some basics—things that are so basic you have to wonder why we even have to mention them. But we do. You'll see in a minute:

1. Come to the networking meeting with a clear agenda and having done some deep homework about the company or the industry or profession. If you're really interested in your networking contact's world (enough to possibly seek a job in it), demonstrate that by knowing something about that world before going into the meeting. And have some good questions to ask that reflect a true passion for the field or understanding of the industry, especially in terms of its current issues.

2. Be gracious. Arrive a little early, keep the meeting focused, and leave when you promised the meeting would be over. Show your networking partner that you respect his time. Your own time deserves to be respected as well. At the end of the meeting, make sure you ask him if you can return the favor in any way.

3. Don't badmouth other players in the industry or profession. You never know who this person knows (or plays tennis with).

4. Have a clear idea of how this person might help you. In Chapter 18, "Your Power Tool: The Targeted Opportunity Profile," we introduce you to the targeted opportunity profile (TOP), which will be your most valuable icebreaker and networking tool. Don't just ask some vague question about who's hiring whom. Engage your networking partners in helping you fill it out. Give them the chance to contribute to your ongoing project.

5. This is the big one: Send a thank you note or email. And then keep your networking partners in the loop as you

move forward with their referrals. This seems like an obvious step, but we are constantly shocked at how often people don't send thank you notes. Sure, we get busy. And time gets away from us, especially when we're busy looking for work. But if you want your network to continue to care about your progress, show you care about their help. Follow up, follow up, follow up.

In fact, follow up three times. You're not just networking; you're building a network. A well-constructed network is like a fishing net, which is only as good as its knots, which you are tying one knot at a time. Each knot takes these steps:

1. A well-run meeting.
2. An immediate thank you note or email, asking permission for you to keep them current with your progress.
3. Thank you emails that you send to their referrals upon meeting with them, as well as another note back to your original contacts to let them know how the referral meetings went.

Build your network with as many excellent knots as you possibly can. But keep in mind that quantity alone is not quality. If it were, all those LinkedIn members—the ones with 500 contacts which then add up to millions upon millions in their so-called network—would have fantastic careers.

This probably isn't the first time you've thought that maybe it's time for you to do some networking. And it most likely won't be the last. But we hope that this networking approach will help you build that network that will see you through your entire career, only to continue to grow with quality knots.

The best thing that you can do:
Open your mind to a different kind of networking model that requires a spirit of adventure and more direct personal responsibility for the outcome.

The worst thing that you can do:
Think that you are in deep trouble just because you focused so hard on doing a quality job for your last employer that you were not the networking maven you should have been.

The first thing you should do:
Set up a routine so that your three-step follow-up process is in place, and you will never forget to send a thank you note again.

Out of Town, But Not Out of Mind

They shut down his product. But because the company had routinely offered a retention bonus to make sure the product shipped on time, Ralph was sitting on a nice little chunk of cash. He and his wife had always dreamed about spending up to a year traveling around the world. However, Ralph worried that his network would go stale while he was gone. In the weeks before he and his wife embarked, he collected all of his contacts in one database and printed self-adhesive address labels of everyone in his network. During his travels, Ralph bought postcards, applied the preprinted labels, and dropped the cards in the mail. By the time he hit Australia, about a month before he was due to return home, he sent a quick email from a cyber café to several contacts requesting a time to meet after he returned. By the time he returned, rested from his travels, his network was primed and ready to help. Ralph was surprised at how often cards from his travels were displayed prominently in his network contacts' offices.

CHAPTER 12

How to Network Without Sounding Phony, Lame, or Desperate

A h. Networking. The very thought makes you feel like a teenager all over again, doesn't it? But not in a good way, probably. Back then, it seemed as though the world was divided into two groups: the people who could magnetize friends without even trying (they were the ones with the fun weekends planned), and those who couldn't no matter how hard they tried (they were the ones who didn't).

Now, when it comes to the talent of building and keeping large networks, the world is still divided into two groups: those who seem to know just everyone, and those who don't. On the surface, networking seems to come easily to the successful crowd. But the truth is that, when it comes to using networking specifically to look for a job, hardly anyone does it very well. They confuse networking with making friends. And the most sensitive of job searchers despise networking for the way it makes them feel:

Phony: You feel phony because you equate networking with social superficiality. Over your entire life, you've taken pride in the fact that you have a select circle of true, authentic friends. You've watched other people "work the room," slick, backslappers, ultra-extroverted folks who never seem to focus on the person in front of them because they're busy scanning the room to see who else is there. Now you're in the position of having to build up your circle of contacts at hyper-speed, and you want to do this in a way that's consistent with your own values and nature. Heaven help you if you're an introvert, because networking the way you've seen it done so far will be agony. How many times can you pretend to be interested in the family pictures on people's desks?

Speaking of inauthentic, what about that opening that so many career counselors advise you to start with? *"I'm not looking for a job, I just want to get some advice from you."* No one buys that line anymore… if they ever did. You certainly never did. So why punish yourself by following bad advice? Especially when it causes you to hate yourself later.

Lame: If you hate networking, chances are you don't do it well. Conversations stall into awkward silences. You suddenly can't think of a single thing to say that will pull the discussion out of the mud. You just know the person you're talking to is beginning to run mental scripts to get out of this one-on-one with you, starting with, "Oh my gosh! Look at the time!" And frankly, you can't blame them. You'd get out of this conversation with you, too, if it didn't defy the laws of nature.

Desperate: Let's face it. You need a job. Fast. If you didn't, would you even be doing this networking thing? Probably not. You'd be too busy working. So, to be truly authentic in your networking style, you'd have only one question for people: "Do you know of any openings? No? Okay. Well. Uhm. Thanks." And then you move on to the next person, with the same question.

You're too classy to actually handle networking that way. But you know desperation is still exuding from your pores like pheromones. And as much as you try to broadcast a positive, upbeat, in-control demeanor, everyone knows you're on the job hunt. And time's a-wastin'.

Maybe you're also feeling like you deserve to be on the receiving end of some divine retribution. You think back to when you were completely busy with a demanding job and some poor guy called you out of the blue to ask for a net-working appointment. He probably said something like, "I'm not looking for a job in your company, I just want to ask for some advice." And you saw right through that, thinking to yourself, "What a lame-o." So you said no.

And now you're walking your own mile in that guy's shoes. And to make matters worse, you would really like to give that very same guy a call because you heard he's landed in a great company.

Networking takes a lot of time, initiative, energy, and stamina. So you need an approach to networking that's not going to make you feel phony, lame, or desperate. Or judged. Or patronized. Or rejected. You don't want to feel as though you're using people as stepping stones to your next job. And you don't want to put yourself and the people you talk to through the phony dance of pretending that that's not what you're looking for anyway.

You want a networking approach that's driven by integrity, truly valuable conversations that bring value to both you and the people you're talking to, and that will ultimately help you create and sustain a powerful and effective network that will endure your entire career (and put you in a great position to help others along the way).

It just requires a mental shift in perspective and attitude about networking and your role in the process. Throughout the rest of this book, we show you how to create a networking plan that will help you achieve this great vision for yourself and your career. And then to turn your networking efforts into solid job offers—culminating into the one job that you say yes to. But for now, let's start with a basic foundation.

Vina Galetto, a friend of Duncan's, has a formula that she calls the Three B's of High-Integrity Networking. True to her own generous nature, she's happy to let us bring it to you:

1. **Be there.** This means that you must start by being there for yourself and show up. Set goals. Understand how networks work, keep good records, and track where you are in the process. Celebrate successes along the way; don't just wait until you've landed a job. Keep in mind that good networking expands as you learn of additional opportunities and introductions. If you find your list shortening and your circles contracting, recalibrate your efforts to start expanding again (we'll show you how soon... right now, we just want to focus on your attitude and perspective).

2. **Be yourself.** Understand who you are in the absence of a particular job title. Remember that your capabilities as a professional have not been taken away simply because you're temporarily unemployed. Don't let the absence of a corporate business card rob you of your identity and intrinsic value. It's just card stock. It's just a moment in time. You own your career and your professionalism. No one can take that away.

   Engage with people in an authentic way. Keep in mind that the HJM networking meeting is always a conversation between peers. You're not there to pitch your product to someone with all the power to buy what you have to sell. You're there to compare notes with a professional colleague. So be a listener first. Curious people get the most out of networking conversations because they keep in mind that they're there to learn, not to sell.

   When you do speak, speak with them the way you would want to be spoken with. Get really comfortable with who you are and what you bring to the marketplace. Get comfortable, even, with aspects of your past that you might be ashamed of. If you are out of work involuntarily, you can anticipate some questions that might rattle your confidence. Know what those uncomfortable questions might be and have your answers—authentic answers—ready to deploy. These questions might be:

"So, how come you've been out of work for as long as you have?"

"Why were you selected to leave the organization? What happened?"

"Why didn't you go back and get more education?"

"What are your strengths and weaknesses?"

"Tell me about a time when you failed. What did you learn from that experience?"

You may never hear those questions asked of you—especially when you own the meeting agenda, as we're going to teach you. But just knowing that you have a solid, prepared answer will give you the confidence to move ahead into new networking conversations with strangers.

3. **Behave yourself.** It's amazing how small the world is, especially when you're pulled over at the side of the road, handing over your license and registration. It may be unfair—when you could use just one break in life right now—but you have to be operating on a much higher standard of behavior than that slob next door who is still pulling down a paycheck. People will be seeing you, even when you're not looking. You may not have much control over your career prospects right this very minute, but you can control whether you have that "oh one little drinkee more won't hurt" drink. Stay away from parties that mix cameras with alcohol. (And we don't need to tell you about those pictures on social networking sites, do we?)

Be nice to everyone you meet. Be gracious, even to that driver who snagged that parking spot you had been politely waiting for. And don't assume that just because that was a stranger you just vented your rage on that you'll never see that person again. Right now, you're in the business of meeting strangers. And you don't want to put "extend sincere apology" on your list of things to do to "be yourself."

Behaving yourself also involves being generous with *your* time and resources. You may be out of a job right now, but you aren't flat out of recommendations, references, and referrals to give others. Say yes to people who reach out to you for a networking meeting. Even if you're thinking that the people in your immediate circles can't help you, maybe they can help that person. Your generosity to them might help dilute any feelings of scarcity you might be beating yourself up with about your own search. You'll be helping both of you more than you can know.

The best thing you can do:
Change your attitude about networking. It's about meeting your colleagues, not banging a tin cup and begging for work.

The worst thing you can do:
Send that flaming email about that rotten boss you had, the lame coworkers you had, and that the whole stinking world is unfair.

The first thing you can do:
Google yourself to see what your image is online. Clean up any messy evidence of a regrettable evening—or entire past.

A Gift from the Sea

Jim always made sure his appearance was impeccable. It was in keeping with his stature as a corporate CFO, even though he was now out of a job. Being laid off (when his company bought another, the other CFO was kept on) didn't stop him from pursuing the sport he loved best, though. So on the weekends, he trained as a triathlete—running, biking, and rough-water swims in the Pacific Ocean. On one Saturday, he was competing with about 2,000 contests in a particularly challenging rough-water swim—the kind that leaves swimmers exhausted, often with bruises and bloody noses from the crowded thrashings of their competitors. And his appearance was the last thing on his mind.

After the race, Jim emerged from the water and stumbled to beach, worn out and battered. Then he spotted another competitor he knew also coming out of the water. While catching their breath, Jim and the fellow competitor filled each other in on their lives. Jim told him about the acquisition and his subsequent search for a new position as a CFO. "Really?" said his friend, "One of my clients is looking for a CFO, and he's also in the swim. In fact, he wasn't that far behind me." Just at that moment, the CEO joined them. And so they got acquainted, looking decidedly worse for the experience they had just shared. They agreed to meet the next week—the unspoken assumption being that they would look significantly better next time.

That meeting resulted in a job offer, which Jim happily accepted.

CHAPTER 13

Make Your Networking Strictly Business

When you're conducting an HJM research meeting, you don't need lunch or "can I buy you a cup of coffee?" as an excuse to seek out a conversation with someone you have targeted as a good source of career information. This is a business meeting (not a social encounter) and should be treated with the uninterrupted focus that any business meeting should be given.

First of all, let's get this whole lunch/coffee date question out of the way right now. Here's what's wrong with that approach:

- **Lunch only happens once a day, and how much coffee do you really need?** Somewhere in modern society, we have come to believe that when we want someone's attention, we should offer the opportunity to eat. During the business week, that means lunch. But if you restrict your networking conversations to only lunches, that means that you will only give yourself five appointments a week (assuming that the person you want to meet is even available for lunch). The alternative is coffee. So, you hold court at the local café and keep it flowing. All morning and into the afternoon. That's really not very good for you. And how attractive do you think you are when you're strung out on a day's worth of caffeine?

- **It takes too long to settle down.** An hour's lunch appointment can easily become a two-hour commitment away from the office for your lunch partner. There's leaving the office, getting in the car, finding the restaurant, waiting until your name is called, finding the table, checking the menu, not wanting to get started with the meat of the conversation until after you've ordered. A lot of precious time is wasted with no long-term benefits.

- **Eating venues are noisy and disruptive.** Restaurants and cafés are full of noise. Clanging flatware, crashing plates, hissing espresso machines, waitstaff who introduce themselves by name before telling you about the specials at great, poetic length. Waitstaff who come back with the mile-long pepper mill. Waitstaff who come back yet again with the parm and the micro-plane and grate and grate and grate until you want to say, "You know what? Go away." But you don't. For obvious reasons.

- **You will worry later about your table manners.** You're not making any money right now, so if you're going to spend $20 to $30 on a decent, impressive lunch, you're going to actually eat it. But then, you wonder later if maybe you were talking with your mouth full. And was that smidge of broccoli up front and center on your teeth throughout the entire lunch? What about that spot on your best tie? Did it come from today's lunch or Monday's lunch? Have you been wearing that all week long?

- **Tabletops are tiny.** As you will see in a few chapters from now, you're going to need plenty of room to spread out in the HJM conversation. And you just can't when you're reorganizing the salt, pepper, 35 different brands of sweetener, candle, and bud vase. There's one restaurant in Santa Fe where the tabletops are so cluttered with accoutrements that Martha routinely clears the deck by putting it all on the floor. She doesn't conduct business meetings there.

- **The small matter of the check.** Who pays? Is it Dutch? You're the one who extended the invitation. So, whether it's coffee or a full lunch, by all rights, you should be the one to pay—especially when you've made it clear that your lunch date is doing you a huge favor to helping you push your job search forward. Multiply the price of the lunch by two (people at the table) and then by five (days in the week) and then by four (weeks in a month) and we're beginning to get into some serious numbers here. Just when you really should be brown-bagging it. (And we're not even figuring in the price of all those high-end coffees for two both in the mornings and afternoons.)

Of course, if your comfortably employed lunch partner has any class, he or she would recognize that the magnanimous thing to do would be to offer to pick up the check. But, how humiliating would that be for you? Suddenly, you're no longer colleagues exploring possibilities and ideas together. You are on the receiving end of a free lunch. Are you an equal? No.

Food shouldn't factor in your networking strategy at all. In fact, when we look for the essential ingredients of an ideal HJM networking meeting, food is most emphatically eliminated from the list. These ingredients, however, make the cut:

Flexible: You are available to make an appointment any time of the day. When the person you want to meet has an hour on the calendar, grab it.

Convenient: It must be convenient for the person you want to meet. Ideally, that person shouldn't even have to get up from his or her desk to spend an hour with you.

Efficient: You're there for exactly one hour. Get started right away and finish on time.

Comfortable: If the person you want to meet is comfortable, you're comfortable.

Respected: This is an hour when no one should take phone calls and other interruptions. Emails shouldn't be checked. Casual drop-bys by coworkers should be discouraged with a closed door.

Easy access to important information: When your networking partner is sitting at his desk, he's going to have all the important names and phone numbers of additional people you should meet within reach. There may be something you want to show (or see) on the Web. That's doable at the desk. A quick phone call to introduce you to a powerful networking connection? An article in a file folder? A white paper to look up and print? Someone right down the hall who really needs to meet you *right now?* So easy if handled at the person's office.

To recap: When it comes to conducting HJM networking meetings, restaurants = inadvisable; the person's office = absolutely ideal.

But, there may come a time when it's a bad idea to meet at that person's office. Maybe it takes too long to get through security in the lobby. Or the person's office is a pigsty. Or the coworkers are buttinskys. You still don't have to restrict yourself to mealtimes and menus.

Try a lovely park near the person's office. Even though it smacks of a spy story (you know, meeting outside where you can't be bugged or overheard), Duncan says that some of his clients' most pleasant and productive meetings have taken place in lovely parklike settings. Everyone has the chance to get outside, take in a little fresh air and sunshine.

Join the person on a volunteer excursion, requesting that she set aside some time to talk to you about your career research. Working in the San Diego area, one of Duncan's clients drove to Mexico with a person he wanted to network with. The volunteer mission of the day was to construct some housing for a poor community across the border. There was the car ride down and the ride back up (not to mention all that time in backed-up traffic at U.S. Customs) to get acquainted, compare notes, and brainstorm possibilities.

Whatever venue you pick, there is every reason why you can be upfront about your objectives for the meeting. No one is expecting you to be coy, hoping to cunningly slide in a conversation around who might be hiring between the endive and the iced tea.

Everyone is busy, even those who sincerely want to help you on your job search path. Their time is much more valuable than the gift of a lunch or the price of a cup of coffee. Make your meeting as simple and straightforward as you can. You'll be saving time. You'll be saving money. You'll be saving calories. And you'll be helping them help you.

The best thing you can do:
Cluster networking meetings geographically to save time and gas.

The worst thing you can do:
Keep bbbbbuying those ddddouble ssshot espresso ddddrinks!

The first thing you should do:
Make your next appointment one that doesn't involve food.

$35 and Nothing to Show for It

Marion had just walked out of the women's professional association. It was well attended, and the speakers included a CEO, a consultant, and a CFO talking about career issues for women in leadership. Of course, much of the discussion was about keeping a career going in a tough economy. Networking was key, the panel agreed. Heard that one before. The topic was interesting and certainly germane to her out-of-work situation. She did reconnect with two past coworkers. They were also out of work, although one was trying her hand at networking. At her table, there were three salespeople looking for business, two other people looking for work, and one person on some sort of spiritual journey. Thirty-five bucks. Down the drain. And that was just this one lunch.

She added her expenses in her head. This week she attended two breakfast meetings like this (the "Dawn Patrol" as her old coworker described it), at least three Starbucks meetings (although one was a weekly get together with friends), and two lunches. More than $100 and 18 hours and 3 new connections—all of whom offered to take a look at her resumé.

What she really wants, she concluded, is a chance to have an in-depth uninterrupted conversation with people who have the power to hire. She vowed to herself to try to improve the odds, and reduce the time and expense. When she got home, she emailed one of the three new connections. "It was good to meet you the other day," she wrote, "I would really value some time to meet with you and talk more about my search and what's going on in the industry. Is there a good time for you next week?" The reply, "The only time I could meet for lunch is three weeks from now, would that work?" Marion's response, "I was thinking we could make this more convenient for you. How about I come by your office? It will save time and give us more options. How does the later part of the week look?"

The reply: "That can work. How about 10:00 a.m. next Thursday?"

Cost = $0.

Value? A lot higher than the "Dawn Patrol."

CHAPTER 14

Seven Essential Signs That Your Networking Is Working

You're looking for a new job. That's established. And while networking, you're supposed to be completely upfront with everyone you meet about the fact that you're looking for a new job. That way, you're not being *phony*. And you're not supposed to be pinning your hopes on each and every one of your networking meetings that *this one could be the one* that nets you the job offer of your dreams (hence taking care of the *lame* and *desperate* concerns).

Let's be realistic here. In your heart of hearts, you probably still wish that each one of these meetings will instantly morph into a "you're hired!" conversation. (Yes, it happens sometimes.) But, because it's all about finding a new job, you are more likely to uncover new opportunities as a result of networking targeted at the hidden job market (HJM). In addition, you will uncover more positions that were posted but you did not know about in other industries and with new career possibilities. This means that you will up your game to another level of networking beyond the tired approach of "Hey, umm, have you heard of any jobs out there and would you pass my resumé around to someone important?" You can do better.

HJM meetings are, in fact, so valuable that we want you to get the best return on investment for your time and effort as well as the best return on investment for the person you are meeting with. This means that you will have a better quality discussion that will not only give you better insights to opportunities and where they are, but will cement each person in your ever-expanding network as a permanent link—a link over which information will flow and connections will be made, not just for now, but throughout the future of your job search and career.

It doesn't take too much additional effort to make this work. Ironically, though, most jobseekers are clumsy about it, squandering many networking connections with lame meetings, poor follow-through, and thoughtless comments. This is because jobseekers who have networking meetings that do not translate into opportunities think that the meetings were "dead ends" and treat them as such. Nothing could be further from the truth.

So, if every one of these HJM research meetings isn't about ever so imperceptibly sliding into job interview mode, what good are they anyway? How do you know whether an HJM research meeting is successful, if landing a job isn't Job One? You'll know the HJM research meeting is successful by how it moves you forward:

1. **You had the chance to talk about what your objective is.** Your focus should be on what you want to do, not what you've done in the past. What are your goals? What does an ideal job look like to you?

2. **You've learned something new about your industry, profession, or career objectives.** By the end of the meeting, you'll have some new insight or data point to think more deeply about. This will make you wiser as you consider your options and a more impressive conversationalist at your next HJM research meeting.

3. **You didn't get resumé advice.** The resumé didn't even come out. Why? Because you didn't bring it, of course.

4. **You didn't lose focus because one smart person gave you bad advice.** Sometimes, really smart people give really bad advice. "It can't be done," they say, "that's just the way it is." Or, "If you want to change professions altogether, you'll have to start at the bottom again." The first time you hear

this, it might give you insight into how to describe your background or your skills in a different way to show a better fit to your target job. Or it will give you important information about how to achieve your goals; gaps you might have to close. If you hear it three times, it might be time to take stock of your options.

5. **The meeting started and concluded on time.** This is more than an issue of punctuality. It shows that you were the one in control of the agenda. You started with focus, and you didn't let the meeting peter out to a boring close. You're not left with the feeling that maybe you were given the bum's rush because you just couldn't bring yourself to depart. The meeting started respectfully and concluded with dignity, with you in charge the entire time.

6. **You left with at least two new contacts to pursue.** Remember that one of the key purposes of the HJM networking process is to break into new clusters of people. And each HJM research meeting is your key to clusters that you haven't yet investigated. When you have an HJM research meeting, you've spent one of your contacts, so at the least, you need to replenish your stock with one new contact name. But, a successful HJM research meeting will generate one to replace the one you spent, plus one (an heir and a spare, so to speak).

Real progress happens when your contact gives you three to six new people who they think will be really help move your job search along. And they will make personal introductions right then and there (which they can because they're at their desk, not sitting in a noisy restaurant).

Will all your meetings be so spot-on? Probably not. And that's okay. You're prospecting. As you get more experience, you'll get better at your prospecting techniques, whether it is becoming more articulate about what your goals are, or timing the meeting to close at that 60-minute mark, or confidently asking for suggestions of additional people you should meet—without feeling as though you're being phony, lame, or desperate.

Overall, as you conclude your meetings, you want to know that your prospects have expanded by at least two, three, or even more. If that's not happening, look at this list and see where you need to improve your technique.

7. **Your contact wants to stay informed of your progress.** Even though you have spent one contact in the HJM research meeting, you haven't really actually lost that contact. Promise to report on the outcomes from the new connections generated during this meeting. You must loop back to each one of your HJM meeting partners at least three times:

- Of course, a thank you note for his time (but we didn't have to tell you that, did we?).

- Follow up within 48 hours with an update on what you've done with the information that that person gave you, including news on whether you were able to set up appointments. (This could be a time when your meeting partner volunteers to drop an additional line of introduction, in case you're having trouble making the connection.) It's also a good idea to include an article or link to an interesting story with your follow-up, so that you are bringing value to your HJM meeting partners as much as you're asking for their help.

- After you meet with anyone your contact referred you to, send him another note simply letting him know you met with the referral, report on positive outcomes from the meeting, and remember to thank him again for the introduction.

That's it. Just three follow-up contacts will assure that you tie this person permanently to your network. And they will think of you first when they hear of new opportunities that might be just right for you.

By doing it this way, you differentiate yourself from other people in the job market. You would think that this basic courtesy would be extended by everyone on the search. The reality? Few people ever loop back to their contacts other than to say, "I haven't found a job yet, hear of anything else out there?" In fact, few people ever bother to thank the person who actually gave them the lead that resulted in the job.

But that's not you. Is it?

The best thing you can do:
After each HJM meeting, do a self-assessment. How did it go? What will you do better next time?

The worst thing you can do:
Blow off the basic courtesies of sending a sincere thank you note, just because a meeting did not turn out the way you had hoped.

The first thing you should do:
Start a system to track whom you have spoken with, whom they referred you to, and whether you followed up. And then whether you have looped back to the originator of the referral to say thanks.

What Gets Measured Is What Gets Done

After nine months of unproductive job search, Susan, a laid-off manufacturing manager, knew she was in trouble because she was running out of cash fast. She had been searching, networking with friends, attending networking events, and looking online. But, there were no postings in her field at all.

As she reviewed her efforts, she realized she needed to be brutally honest with herself about her job search activities and their lack of effectiveness at this point. Using the disciplines she learned in manufacturing, she began to measure both the quantity and the quality of her activities, to determine if her search was on track.

Each day, she recorded the calls she made and emails she sent. She also plotted the results, how many calls or emails got responses, and whether she successfully set a meeting as a result. She evaluated the meeting based on whether she achieved her core objectives, giving herself a score of 1 to 5 in each category. Finally, she measured the count of new organizations, target contacts, and job opportunities she uncovered. What she learned was that she needed to boost the quality of each interaction.

Each day and each week, she set new goals, and noticed an immediate increase of opportunities. The best part of all: Each day, she had the satisfaction of seeing progress. A month later, she had her job.

STEP 4

POWER UP YOUR JOB SEARCH

CHAPTER 15

Opening Day: How to Organize Your HJM Search Campaign

If there's one good thing to say about the traditional job search approach, it's this: It's really easy to stay organized. First of all, you have tons of time because you aren't that busy anyway. Second, all those automated job search concierges will be delivering job postings directly to your computer—just as they're doing for millions of other job searchers. Third, how organized do you have to be to stand for hours in line at job fairs, marveling at the way your fellow line-standers are dressed? Instead of having your pick of "gobs of jobs" at these events, you're watching gobs of slobs in line ahead of you. Despite your obvious advantage of being appropriately dressed, you leave the event thinking, "That's one morning of my life I'll never get back." See how easy it is? Very straightforward. Lots of waiting. Very passive. Lousy results.

The HJM search campaign takes a more proactive effort, a different approach to organization, and initiative. But, it's worth it—even if the bottom-line promise is that you'll never have to go to one of those job fairs again. The HJM search requires a shift in your perspective about how the job market works and how to proactively organize your activities.

In the traditional job search approach, jobseekers tend to think of the job market as a static pond with a set number and selection of published jobs. As the economy suffers, there is a smaller pond and more jobseekers until the pond looks like opening day of fishing season. For every job taken, there is one less job opportunity for you. But, the reality is that the market looks more like a stream than a pond. Sure, a stream is bigger some times than other times, but there is a constant flow of new opportunities. The choice, of course, is to passively wait for opportunities to come by (along with everyone else) or work your way upstream to the sources of opportunities where the real action is.

Because *you* are not going to wait for just the published opportunities that come by, you need to organize your activities to generate new prospects, ideas, introductions, and even solid opportunities. And you've got to have a system to capture and organize them all. The best approach is to borrow from the way successful salespeople manage their opportunities: They make sure that their opportunity stream is constantly flowing. Their operating metaphors? The funnel and the pipeline.

For salespeople (and you), it's important to keep that stream constantly flowing through the funnel, constantly adding new opportunities and ideas into the system so that you always have something to do or someone to call. The ultimate goal is, of course, to find a job. But when you're using the funnel approach, you measure your success on a daily basis in terms of how well you're filling your funnel. They take time to build up, and you'll have constant stream of opportunities in motion. So don't let the flow stop; otherwise, you'll have to start all over again, which is demoralizing beyond words. The flow keeps your process moving through the funnel. And the funnel helps you transform the wide universe of possibilities that come in at the top into a narrow, defined, and refined selection of real job opportunities as they emerge from the spout and into the pipeline—and one of those opportunities will become the one job for you. (And some backup positions in case the "one" job falls through.)

Let's start from the broad mouth of the funnel, which is where the entire process begins. And we call that process SPOT:

- **Suspects.** Start filling the funnel with suspects: organizations, industry segments, industries that serve industry segments, or companies in a geographical region that you've identified as possibilities. You don't have to know anything about these organizations or companies right now other than the fact that they meet basic criteria that's important to you. You're just collecting names of these organizations right now. You always want at least 200 names at this stage (the wide end of your funnel).

- **Prospects.** The funnel starts to narrow now. This level is filled with prospects that have begun to emerge from your suspects list. (Don't forget to keep filling the suspects level.) Your prospects list is made up of organizations that would be qualified to hire someone like you. You're just looking for companies that may already have people in jobs like the ones you might want. (You're not looking for companies with specific openings.) When you identify these companies, put them in your prospects level, even if you hear that they have a hiring freeze, never hire, don't hire, only promote from within, or you've heard bad things about the organization. If they have employees like you or are likely to one day hire someone like you, they're a prospect. Your goal is to have 75 to 100 prospects in this level of your funnel at all times. Keep replenishing this level, because this is where possible jobs begin to emerge for you.

- **Opportunities.** These are known job openings that are perhaps similar to jobs that would interest you and for which you have decided to apply. There may be publicly announced openings of formally defined jobs that meet your criteria, or you've had conversations with people inside prospect companies that could lead to the creation of a specially designed job just for you. What's important here is that these opportunities aren't long shots. They're real possibilities for you to consider. It will take a while to build up this level of the funnel, but eventually, you'll want to achieve and sustain five to ten opportunities at all times, so you never have to make a compromised choice out of desperation. They become part of your pipeline after you are in the second round of interviews.

- **Targets.** This level is made up of people with the ability to hire. You know who these people are, their names, and possibly their contact information. They are *not* in HR, unless you're building a career in human resources. They are hiring managers scattered throughout the organizations that you have identified in your suspects, prospects, and opportunities levels. Depending on the job you are shooting for, there may be more than one target in an organization. In fact, there might be more than one division at separate locations with more than one target in your hometown.

Your ultimate job opportunity—the one that you will successfully negotiate to a firm offer that you can say yes to—can come out of any level in the funnel. But, when you organize your search with the funnel model in mind, you'll be constantly aware of how it's being filled from the suspects level on down. Once you have it fully flowing, constantly ask yourself whether you have 200 suspects, 75 to 100 prospects, and at least 5 opportunities that are worth pursuing or are being developed.

As for your targets, this is where the funnel expands out again. You want to be constantly collecting names of people to know in your career community. Because you are committed to your profession and career development, you want to be associated with the best of the best in your field. They'll become lifelong members of your network, and they may have the power to hire you either now or some other time. Or you might have the chance to hire them. This is a lasting advantage that your career will enjoy years after you close this book.

The best thing you can do:
Expand your search of prospects to include organizations that are in your industry but are not based in your community (so they miss the local company listings). They might have a small local office or virtual teams. If you find they could hire people in your area, make them a suspect.

The worst thing you can do:
Once you find a couple of opportunities, stop working your other suspects, prospects, and targets. Do not stop until after you cash your first paycheck.

The first thing you should do:
Continue adding names to your list.

It's Just Good Territory Management

Ann sold high-powered computers for scientific and engineering applications in Seattle and Alaska. She learned early in her career that the key to success as a salesperson was to build a pipeline of opportunities to feed a steady stream of sales. She also knew that computer deals that were valued at the same dollar amount as her desired salary would take about three months to close.

She applied the same pipeline logic when she decided to change careers after taking some time off to have a family and complete her MBA. She started the search in December and set the goal of three offers by March 31. Her research revealed 85 "suspect" companies. Through networking and direct applications, she uncovered nine opportunities. Of those, she rejected two as a bad fit. One didn't pan out as being a true opening. Two hiring managers said they needed someone with different skills. And four offered her a position. She accepted her position one week before her goal.

CHAPTER 16

Backdoor Research to Uncover HJM Targets

When you start imagining yourself exploring the hidden job market, you might think that success is reserved for the most extroverted and energetic networkers out there. If you're naturally introverted, you might think you're out of luck, yet again.

Actually, you're in luck. While it's true that you're going to have to meet a lot of strangers (with perhaps a handful of truly strange strangers along the way), your real advantage will be your ability to come up with creative approaches to researching the companies that are potential suspects, prospects, and even opportunities. This is going to take some ingenuity, curiosity, and some detective work on your part. And most of that initial work is solitary research. Lucky you. But, even with the growing popularity of online social networking sites, such as LinkedIn, Xing, Plaxo, Twitter, and Facebook, eventually, you have to get out of the house.

You have to be willing to go beyond the job boards, the locally advertised companies, the companies that are the darlings of your local economy, even the denizens of your local area's Best Employers list. You don't have to have the research skills of a reference librarian. Although if you befriend one, he or she will show you how much fun it really can be to dig, letting one clue lead you to five more possibilities. And if you find a reference librarian who whispers over the vertical files, "Oh my gosh! This is so *cool!*," you really hit the jackpot. But, you can still do this yourself.

If you like to solve mysteries, you're going to be well ahead of the competition—all those people who are just passively searching online job banks. If you don't like mysteries or puzzles, start with these suggestions and see if you might develop a taste for exploring. It's an intellectual challenge, to be sure. But, the reward is uncovering deep wells of opportunities that never make it to the traditional job marketplace. And you'll be enjoying your one-on-one HJM research meetings while everyone else is at home filling out yet another online application.

Let's start with *lists*. The natural inclination is to check out your local list of best companies to work for. And if you happen to live near one of the companies that appear on *Fortune* magazine's annual collections of best companies to work for or most admired companies, put it on the list. But don't get too excited; all may not be what it appears to be on the inside. And don't automatically think your neighborhood companies who make local lists are little working paradises. Not every location rigorously manages the selection process for their list. And the "frequent fliers" of those annual lists could either be powerful players in local politics or have figured out how to circumvent the judging process in myriad ways, including hiring public relations firms that specialize in putting together annual campaigns for the contest. We would never go so far as to say that all companies that appear on these lists have found ways to work the system a bit. Just make a note of the companies on these Best Employers lists (particularly the ones that appeal to you for other reasons). And don't stop digging.

All sorts of other available lists can give you additional names of likely company candidates. Your local business newspaper probably publishes an annual "book of lists," which features your area's major employers by size, by industry, by public sector versus private sector, and so forth. Depending on your particular newspaper publisher, you can sometimes get the annual list for free when you subscribe to the paper. (Since you're looking for a job, you might consider subscribing anyway.)

Here's a list of other lists:

- **Membership lists.** These would include your local chamber of commerce and your professional association memberships. Also consider obtaining the membership lists of professional and trade associations that are tangential to your own profession. Sometimes, these lists are confidential, but a member might share them with you, or you can start by gathering the names of the officers of the association (president, vice president of membership, programs, promotions, legal affairs, editor of the newsletter, and so forth), which usually are easily found online. If you can afford the dues, join the associations that are essential to your profession or industry. The advantages of membership usually extend far beyond simply having access to confidential lists. The first one being, of course, that membership in the leading professional organization demonstrates your sincere commitment to the field. You don't want to have to answer the question, "Why aren't you a member?"

- **Buyers guides.** Every association (including local business groups) has an affiliate group of companies that directly serve the professional members. In fact, to look at it another way, every company is probably a member of at least one affiliate group because of its own marketing strategy. (A potato chip manufacturer, for instance, is likely to be a member of the Snack Food Association to stay current on its industry trends. But, it will also be a member of the National Association of Convenience Stores, to take part in the affairs of one of its major markets.) The buyers guides, which are typically published annually, and often online, will give you lists of companies and consulting firms of all sizes that specifically serve some aspect of your profession, the people who work in your profession, as well as the people who serve your profession.

- **Government lists.** If your community has an economic development department, it will be able to tell you what companies are moving in. Look at the government directories themselves for ideas of what agencies might be moving into town and hiring—or might be contracting with private sector companies that will be hiring to accommodate their new projects or contract awards.

- **Technology directories.** If your profession is technical, there are directories of suppliers of products, hardware, software, user groups, special interest groups, and trade show attendees. If you are an experienced user of a software application, companies that sell the software often are interested in learning about people who already know their software or equipment to help a new customer get started on the system. Are you an expert in a particular area of science? Published papers, science symposium speakers, and conferences can give you clues about organizations and people you should know.

- **Social networking websites.** These sites are great, but they have their drawbacks. They can be great places to reconnect with people you have lost track of. As a result, they may even help you uncover connections that might be great resources for the hidden job market. For example, searching for people who you know who now work or used to work at one of your target employers. But, the demographics tend to favor students, younger working adults, and the few hiring managers who are actively using the sites for their recruitment purposes. Remember that right now your objective is to find people and companies in the position to hire someone with your skills. And online social networking can be a distraction, luring you into banal personal news about new puppies, head colds, new cars, and trips to the supermarket. Use social networking websites, but stay focused on your main job—which is to find a job.

Read the *local business press* in your profession or community, but don't just pursue the headline darlings. If you do, you might just be pursuing companies that have great PR strategies, which, unless you're a PR professional, may not have anything to do with your career objectives. Scan the news-in-brief items to see who has just taken new jobs (which could indicate a vacancy at their previous job or the possibility that a company is expanding a business line that is right up your alley). Watch for new contract announcements—which could indicate that these companies might be growing and bringing on new talent. Also read for the bad news. If a certain company is suffering in your target community or profession, you're going to want to know about that before you take on a new job there.

Read the *trade press*. Don't just limit yourself to the trade media that directly serves your own profession. Read the trade press that serves your customers' professions and industries as well.

Consider *outsourcers*. "Outsourcing" is often confused with "offshoring," where jobs are actually sent abroad. But there are a number of domestic outsourcer companies. And if your role inside an organization is typically considered overhead, there's a very good chance that your expertise is actually a profit center for outsourcers. They'll be very happy to hear from you, as you represent the kind of talent that is their competitive edge.

Watch for other shifts in your industry or profession, where new business models open up opportunities that didn't exist before. For instance, new technologies being introduced into established industries. Bringing "green" processes to old industries, social networking to traditional marketing programs, storage and communications technology to healthcare. There is opportunity every time there is a blend of new technology with old.

Follow the *money*. We've already mentioned the opportunities presented by new government contracts and companies that have announced new initiatives. Each new major opportunity has many ripples that affect associated industries, organizations, and communities. There's also money in business contraction. If the economic news is of initiatives shutting down, rather than opening up, there could be opportunity there for you, as well, if your expertise is driving efficiency and cost-effectiveness.

Monitor the *nonprofits*. The employment marketplace for nonprofits is enormous. Even in tight economic times when money may not be flowing as freely, these organizations still need to get the job done. And they have many of the same administrative functions that for-profit corporations have: IT, operations, facilities, marketing, finance, human resources, you name it. Considering many nonprofits' need to operate on a shoestring, if you have multiple skills to offer them, you may be just the person they need. And they'll pay you well for it. And if this particular nonprofit is serving a cause that's personally important to you, that satisfaction is an added benefit you might not get elsewhere.

Think about how your profession *clusters* with other professions. When you're working to uncover companies that might hire people like you, look for companies that hire people you would be likely to work with. For instance, if you do sales in technical products, look for companies that are advertising for customer service engineers. Those companies also have technical product sales.

Be creative smart, not creative stupid. As we write this chapter, the local and national media is relishing in hurts-so-good stories of once highly paid executives resorting to acts of extreme self-humiliation to land a job. The former executive with the sandwich board marching up and down Madison Avenue, for instance. Or the guy whose wife has her very own website pleading with the world at large to hire her highly accomplished husband. This is not creative smart. They're getting publicity, that's for sure. But are they getting job offers? At this writing, no.

When it comes to creatively uncovering employment opportunities, your key to success is your curiosity—not the extent of your capacity for humiliation. One connection, one idea, one name in the news leads to another and yet another. Expand your understanding of how businesses work and work with each other, and you'll expand your understanding of your own career marketplace.

That's being creative smart.

The best thing you can do:
Ask people in your professional network for lists they may have of organizations and people you might add to your suspect, prospect, and target lists.

The worst thing you can do:
Ignore a slightly outdated printed list because it is not online.

The first thing you should do:
Get a group of friends together to brainstorm possible sources of data and recruit them to spend some time looking to add to your suspects, prospects, opportunities, and targets lists. Thank them.

Beltway Bandit

Alan, a program manager, spent his career working for a number of government contractors and consulting firms surrounding the Washington, D.C., area (nicknamed Beltway Bandits, after the highway encircling the city). No one assumes that these jobs are permanent—they come and go with the turnover of administrations or the launch of new projects. When a contract is awarded, companies hire. When a contract runs out, companies lay off employees. That's the nature of work in Washington. So Alan knows that his success depends as much on his being able to find new jobs as it is for his doing his current job very well.

When Alan looks for a job, he doesn't rely on job boards or even listings in the *Washington Post* or *Washington Times*. He identifies the bidders for government contracts in his area of expertise. His research tools include www.usaspending.gov and www.defense.mil/contracts and other online sites that provide updated information about what companies have successfully landed government projects. New projects could mean a new surge of hiring.

Follow the funding.

CHAPTER 17

Your Resumé Is Not Your Friend

Bill, a colleague of Duncan's, who has been a business executive, a career consultant, and an executive search recruiter, used to say this about resumés: "Resumés are made of paper. And paper is an insulating material." Bill has a point. Whether printed or soft-copy, resumés actually prevent you from really connecting person to person. Connecting with people who can help you with your search. Connecting with people who have the power to hire you.

So, at the risk of sounding like a heretic, resumés, the one document considered essential to every professional job search, can sink your job search and career before it even gets started. Why? Because resumés screen you out more often than screen you in. It's stunning how often HR folk and recruiters use purely arbitrary reasons to screen people out that have little to do with the actual skills to do a job. Unless you're applying for a job as an editor, a typo gets you tossed? A missing date gets you ditched? A gap in employment (while you had children, were ill, or were being a caregiver) was insufficiently explained? A GPA from a school 15 years ago is "too low" despite stunning success in your subsequent career? The type font irritates them? The list of unqualified disqualifiers goes on.

*The real value of a resumé is to **help you** identify and articulate those accomplishments that represent the best of your abilities, motives and fit.* The breakthrough in resumés was the invention of the accomplishment statement. This is a description of what you actually accomplished in your previous jobs, as opposed to simply listing job responsibilities. These accomplishment statements are actually much more important than simply fodder for resumés. They can be used in interviews, and they can illustrate what you do best, what engages you, and what your past employers have most valued about you. Remember how you picked 12 to 15 problems, situations, or opportunities you faced in your career? Now describe these in 1 or 2 sentences (50 to 60 words). Make sure you include the situation, what you did, and the results (the outcome in terms of what your employer cared about most). How much money did your accomplishment save or generate? Did you create a new process that improved customer satisfaction scores? Did you originate an idea that was an industry first? Did you save a customer? Reduce company risk? Thrill the CEO? Even small improvements, which maybe only took a few hours, but had a big impact, can add up. The key is to look for those items that you are most proud of. These accomplishments truly represent your knowledge, your skills, your values, and your ability to work with and through others. Once you finish, add them to your resumé under the appropriate position. You can also use these refined and sharpened accomplishment statements as prompts during actual interviews to help you remember stories and examples of what you do so well.

This is why resumé writing is important. It's not to help you get a job interview. It's to help guide *you* in the process of describing what you do best.

Of course, it does help to have a resumé when you are asked for one. But, even then, your resumé can derail your hidden job market (HJM) search. Here's why:

- **The minute you hand over your resumé, you become a job supplicant.** Remember that when you're conducting HJM research meetings, you're not looking for a job specifically from that company or the person you're talking to. When you bring out your resumé (which you will no longer do after you've finished this book), you're stuck in that awkward, silent trench of time while the person you're meeting with reads over the document and makes a quick yes/no decision about whether you're a likely candidate for a post within the company. That's not what the HJM research meeting is for, and you've just lost control of the agenda.

- **The resumé is about your past, and you're interested in your future.** When you're conducting an HJM research meeting, you don't want your conversation to be about your history. You want your conversation to be about how you can best bring your abilities, skills, and desires to the right company.

- **There's no way a two-page document can capture all you are and all you can be.** If a resumé is brought out in the HJM research meeting, the focus of your conversation is limited to only the two prescribed pages that the so-called experts insist upon for the "ideal" resumé. We are all so much more than our list of most-recent tasks and accomplishments. And the beauty of the HJM research meeting is that we have a chance to explore what other possibilities and potential exist for us. If you want to spend the next two years doing precisely what you were doing the last two years, then maybe it makes sense to bring out your resumé during the HJM research meeting. But when you do, you've transformed a possibility-oriented brainstorming session into a yes/no job interview. And you will have forfeited the benefits of the hidden job market.

- **Too many people spend way too much valuable time obsessing about creating the perfect resumé.** Let's just say: Opinions are like elbows. Almost everyone has at least one. And there are plenty of opinions swirling around the job market as to what constitutes the perfect resumé. For every perfect version of a resumé you create, you're going to find someone to give you helpful advice on how to improve it. When you listen to your friends, or paid "resumé experts," you'll get confused, demoralized, and you'll lose your confidence before you've even clicked "Send" or printed out a stack of these documents. Worse yet, in the HJM meeting itself, if you find that the person you're meeting with spends any time at all suggesting ways you can improve your resumé ("Have you thought about having more white space?"), you've lost precious minutes that should have been focused on more valuable topics, such as the state of the industry, what challenges the company faces, what your own goals are in your overall career.

There is just no upside to obsessing whether the left margin should be an inch or an inch and a half. And once you've committed hours upon hours to revising the resumé, with no positive results of actually getting a job, you are at risk for believing that it's not the resumé that's flawed, it's you. No. It's your resumé. And the fact that you're still depending on it to open doors for you.

- **Your resumé will not highlight your perfect background for the surprisingly perfect job opportunity you discovered in a HJM networking interview.** So there you are, talking to a target manager in a target position and she starts talking about a need she has. The conversation leads to brainstorming about a job possibility, but you realize that the resumé you have with you misses the mark. You need to take some details out and put others in. Easy.

So, why bring a resumé into this meeting at all? You'll only be tempted to hand it over, when you know it's oh-so-wrong. A delay of 24 hours won't disqualify you from consideration for a real job opportunity, should there actually be one that emerges from your meeting.

If the meeting goes as well as we all hope it does, the question about your resumé might come up. Whatever you do, don't have it with you. Just make those changes back home and then send the updated, customized resumé.

Here's how the conversation might go:

Your target: "Wow, it's really been great meeting you! I'm already thinking of several people here in the company who will want to know about your abilities. Do you have your resumé with you?"

You: "You know, based on our conversation, I'm thinking of several aspects of my background that might be of specific value to you. So, I'd like some time to make sure those details are included for your reference. How about if I get it to you first thing tomorrow? This way, you'll also have it as an email attachment that you can forward to your colleagues."

Who is going to say "no" to that?

And, at the very least, you'll be able to get the resumé just right.

The best thing you can do:
Instead of 12 to 15 accomplishments, brainstorm 20. Then, pick your baker's dozen (that's 13, in case you were wondering)—those sweet things that really demonstrate what you do so well.

The worst thing you can do:
Make yourself crazy by endlessly "improving" your resumé. You only want to customize it for a specific job opportunity that you've uncovered during your HJM research meeting.

The first thing you should do:
Once you think your basic resumé is in good shape, get feedback from *only* three people you most respect and who have hired people in positions similar to the one you are targeting. One last tweak and put it aside until you absolutely must use it.

His Resumé Was So Bad It Was Good

It was the last day of a job search workshop. Around the table sat accomplished professionals in a number of functional areas—accounting, engineering, marketing, sales, operations, and human resources. At one point, the facilitator asked participants to share their resumés to get feedback from the group. People pulled out their two-page resumés they had worked hours to prepare. At a distance, they all looked the same: white paper, conservative font, name at the top of the paper. However David's was different. He was in sales, and he was a seasoned professional. He was quiet during most of the workshop, but the appearance of his resumé screamed "unconventional." It was one page, printed in blue ink, had a headline that said "IMPROVE SALES NOW" and a cartoon clip art of a short heavyset man standing in front of a rising sales chart. Hadn't he been paying attention in class?

The group tried to be polite, but they hated it. "It's unprofessional," one said. "I would have to reject it," said the HR person. "Your name is in a typeface that's too small," said the accountant. "The clip art should be clipped out," said the marketing person.

At first, David smiled. Then, he laughed out loud. "I know this resumé violates everything this workshop talks about, but I have to tell you, I have sent this resumé just as it is to five sales managers and I got five interviews in the first week of my job search. I don't think I will change a thing."

The workshop facilitator was intrigued and took a closer look at the resumé. Why would this awful resumé be so effective? The answer was in the core message. David's resumé focused on what sales managers really care about the most. Eight years of beating quota. Eight years of being in the top 10% in sales for the company. Awards for new customers, opening new markets, and growing business. Simply put, his resumé focused solely on what salespeople are supposed to do: improve sales now.

David landed his next job within three weeks (and ahead of his classmates).

CHAPTER 18

Your Power Tool: The Targeted Opportunity Profile

Fans of *The Godfather* are particularly fond of this line: "Leave the gun. Take the cannoli." We're telling you to leave the resumé at home. So. Hmm. What to take with you? Consider the *targeted opportunity profile* (TOP) your cannoli.

A quick refresher on what's wrong with bringing your resumé: It's a work history. It's about what you have done, not necessarily about what you want to do. It insulates you from connecting with people. ("Why should I get to know you? I have your resumé, and that is *everything* I need to know"—in two pages!) It positions you as a job supplicant, rather than as a peer or colleague having a mutually beneficial conversation with another colleague. A resumé invites judgment.

You want a document that invites collaboration, not judgment. And that's exactly what the TOP does for you. The TOP is more powerful than the slickest, most professionally done resumé. It's a living project that evolves over time, as you enlist those you meet with to help you fill it out and build it up. It's a way to quickly bring new people up to speed about your career aspirations and ideas. The TOP also builds on each hidden job market (HJM) research meeting and thus ignites fresh thinking about how to drive your job search forward. It's your tool for making progress and for building your community of contacts along the way.

The best TOP is two or three pages, and has lots of empty boxes that you and your HJM meeting partner fill in together during your meeting. It's an outline of your job objective, a snapshot of the kinds of companies and managers who would most want to hire someone with your skills, and a list of specific, possible employers. It's your common point of focus. And by the time the meeting is over, your TOP has evolved yet again. Don't be surprised if you hear, "Can I have a copy for my own use?" Those you meet with might be so intrigued by the TOP that they make this request. In short, the TOP is a great way to distinguish yourself and build new relationships. You can't exactly say the same thing for resumés.

Expect a lot of scribbling and note taking (done on the paper copy you take to your HJM research meetings). This is a collaborative document, so note taking is socially acceptable in this context. It's part of the nature of an HJM research meeting. (Duncan has created a template for you to download. Just visit www.unlockthehiddenjobmarket.com and follow the links.) Because it's a document designed to be ever-evolving, with additions and subtractions as your job search progresses, you should keep a master copy of your TOP on your computer for your own private reference. When you make a separate TOP that's strictly private, you can make notes to yourself about your HJM meetings and your impressions about the person, whether he or she was helpful, or maybe even whether you found yourself giving that person career advice, instead of the other way around. You can write "what a loser" on your private TOP, without worrying about whether that version of the document might accidentally get circulated. Make sure you color code the file name of your private TOP, and put it in a separate folder, to prevent the risk of accidentally handing it out at your next HJM meeting.

But for now, so that you understand exactly what goes where, let's go over the various elements of the TOP:

- **Name and contact information.** This goes at the beginning of the document. Even though the TOP is primarily for your purposes, you might want to leave a copy of the TOP behind after the HJM meeting. (A quick trip to the photocopier at the end of your meeting will give your contact the same version of the TOP you'll be leaving with.) Your contact might want to think it over or show it to others to get their input. So you want to make sure your meeting partner knows how to get back to you with any fresh ideas that might come up after you have left the building.

- **Objective.** In two to four lines, describe what you would like to do and the value of what you do to the hiring organization. Remember: Think like a hiring manager.

- **Geographic location.** Where do you want to work? If you are open to relocating, where specifically?

- **Possible job titles.** What you're trying to do here is open up possibilities, trigger ideas, and stimulate thinking with the people you meet on your HJM journey. Think about the titles of people who are doing work similar to what you want to do. Don't just aim for vague titles, such as director or vice president. Be specific: business developer, outside sales, account executive. Don't fall in love with any one title. This is strictly for brainstorming. If you need a running start on likely ideas, check out the U.S. Department of Labor's Occupation Information Network (O*NET, http://online.onetcenter.org/)

- **Possible industries.** Be as descriptive as possible about the kinds of industries that most appeal to you. For instance, don't just say "high-tech" or "bio-tech." Say "pharmaceutical companies at commercial stage" or "medical device companies that are in start-up phase" or "post-IPO diagnostic companies."

- **Job titles of hiring authorities.** What would be the titles of a potential boss? Or the boss's boss? Or of their peers? If you're looking for small companies to work for, you might put down "owner" or "partner." Think one or two levels up from you. No further. These are hiring managers directly involved in the work you would be doing. They are not HR, unless you're an HR professional. And do not put "recruiter" or "search firm" on this line—unless you are a recruiter yourself wanting to work for a search firm.

- **Associations and industry trade groups.** These organizations influence and support your profession or industry. Their leaders will be networking contacts. So, you will want to know not only the group's contact information, but also the names of its officers. They are the ones most likely to know the most members of the organization. And remember to look at both national organizations and regional chapters.

- **List of prospects and targets.** This is the list of organizations that you think might hire people like you. Create a separate table for this grouping. Your aim is to have at least 50 organizations on this list, along with a contact person's name, title, phone number, and email address. Also include a box to check when you have actually made contact with these people. (When you show your TOP to your HJM research meeting counterpart, you'll be demonstrating that you're on a truly organized and focused mission.) You don't have all the names and contact information? Perfect. *You actually want empty places and unchecked boxes.* You want the person you are meeting with to help you fill in the blanks. With a quick scan, they can easily identify people and organizations they know and can introduce you to. You'll also cut down on the typical exchange of "have you thought of so and so?" "Yes." "How about so and so?" "Him, too." By scanning your list, your HJM meeting partner will quickly see whom you've met with, and whose names and contact information you still need.

This TOP format tells your meeting partner at a glance whom you've spoken with, what introductions or contact information you still need, and so forth. However, you might want to include one or more of the following three optional segments to round out your document:

- **Funding sources/contracts/programs.** If your job search strategy focuses on organizations that depend on grants and other external sources of operating money, add this category to your TOP.

- **Thought leaders.** These are influential individuals not affiliated with a particular company that might hire you, but who know everyone who is anyone. These people are consultants, authors of books in your field, professors, even reporters, especially those who write for the business section of your local newspaper or magazines.

- **Current list of job openings that could meet your criteria.** When you're out of work, the world feels very large and closed off. But once you get started in the hidden job market, you'll begin to see how small the world really is and how willing people are to share news about openings. One of the best signs that your network is kicking into gear for you is when you start hearing about the same job from multiple sources. By reserving a section of your TOP to job openings you've heard about and the status of your follow-up, you can preempt repeated suggestions about the same job. Your HJM meeting counterparts will see at a glance that you already know about a position they might otherwise mention. And you'll be saved the ungracious moment of telling them, "I already know about that one," which really translates into "what else you got?"

The best thing you can do:
When you share your TOP with anyone, watch the reaction. Do they clearly understand your objective? Are they compelled to add details and update information (which they should be)? If not, figure out why.

The worst thing you can do:
Have an objective that says, "A progressive, well-run organization with a relaxing atmosphere and great pay and benefits where I can use my skills and abilities."

The first thing you should do:
Take your TOP for a spin. Your living document will open doors and expand your network. Tinker with this, not your resumé.

By Face, by Phone, by Email

Should you email your TOP in advance of a meeting? Do you need to be face to face to go over it? What if you live in another city and you can only talk by phone?

Lydia decided to approach the use of the TOP the same way she approached her profession in operations. She simply asked herself, "What works?" After she discovered the TOP and ways it can be used in a search, she experimented with a number of approaches and came up with what worked for her. Over time, Lydia refined her approach to what she found worked best for her. She found that sending an agenda that mentions the TOP immediately before a meeting was helpful, but that sending the TOP itself worked only if people asked her for an advance copy.

"I learned I got the best results when I sat down face to face with people. When face to face, I would watch what people did with the TOP. Did they read it or scan it? Did they write on it? Was there a common question they asked because something was unclear? Did it stimulate ideas and discussion?" Whether face to face or by phone, the best results always came when she carved out time to go over the document with the HJM meeting partner. If she skipped bringing out the TOP, she lost the ideas and leads it could have generated.

The one approach she resolved never to do: Send the TOP on its own, trusting that people would read it on their own. Asking people to look at it and get back to her never worked, as it would just get lost in the shuffle of busy days and competing business demands.

CHAPTER 19

Find the Hot Issues to Uncover the Hot Jobs

You'll be at your best advantage if you "know" the mind of your target employer *before* you actually go into an HJM meeting. How do you do that? Well, you might first want to review Chapter 7, "Think Like a Hiring Manager," and then Chapter 10, "Don't Have the Exact Experience? No Problem!" After that, you want to research issues/opportunities before the meeting so that you can engage in an informed and intelligent conversation when the time comes.

What you really want to understand are the challenges and opportunities (from your target employer's perspective) that might influence hiring decisions. And you want to know the selection criteria and motivators—in *their* language, from *their* perspective—that they use when considering candidates.

This is the other side of the gap analysis. If you understand the needs, challenges, and opportunities from *their* point of view, you can even more effectively close the gap that separates you from your goals. When you start this journey, you investigate what the organizations are trying to accomplish and why. Not just the whole organization, but also the smaller groups: the division, the department, the product team, the customer team, the office team. Your ongoing question is this: Who are the managers with the power to hire, and what will they want you to help them achieve and why?

Sometimes, organizations have it figured out, and they're running smoothly. They will hire you because they need to make the machine bigger, or they need to replace someone who left. More often, especially these days, company leaders are discovering that they need a new vision for their future, with an entirely different set of mission-critical objectives than they had even last year. And so, they are looking out for an entirely different set of skills and talents. In other words, to paraphrase Marshall Goldsmith: What got them here isn't going to get them there. And they might just need you to help them get there.

Successful organizations need to evolve, because they know their competition is evolving. (If your target is a government agency, a school, or a nonprofit, political realities, funding sources, and current issues are evolving.) To adapt, they need to integrate new ideas, new skills, and new capabilities. So, assuming you want to continue building your career by associating with companies that are serious about being competitive players in their marketplace, you need to understand what these issues mean to them. You need to understand the trends and challenges and the opportunities in their world. When you know what their problems are, you will better understand what roles you might play in addressing those problems.

As you research each company or industry, create an issues list that summarizes the problems and opportunities you discover. Pose the essential business questions: Where are they making money? Where are they losing money? What are the latest challenges they're trying to solve given what's going on with technology or their competition or available talent? Are there challenges to the company's supply chain? Could changes in global politics threaten distribution channels? Are there changes in their customers' buying behaviors? Who are their customers, for that matter? Has the customer changed? Has the motive for buying changed? What else might be changing in the company's business environment?

Any one of these questions might point you in the direction of the company's most important problem—one that may need a problem-solving team for which you are a perfect fit.

When, once you are in front of your HJM meeting partner, you ask the question, "How are you handling this?," you might just be opening up an opportunity for yourself.

You want to know what your target company's most important problems are because the most important opportunities lie there as well. But you probably won't find hints to this information in most of the popular business press—or even the local business newspapers (unless you're truly most interested in solving local business problems as the focus of your work).

You'll find industry trends, challenges, and issues by delving just a little deeper into trade magazines, even conference agendas, and the topics of posted presentations. (Thank heavens for PowerPoint presentations posted online; one may actually play a key role in helping you land your next job.) What are these articles and presentations focused on? Any repeating themes that seem to indicate a problem that everyone is passionate about and that just won't go away?

Study the websites of the major consulting firms in your area of interest. What white papers are they publishing? Download free copies or abstracts whenever you can and study their survey results for snapshots of important trends.

Read the analyst reports of industries. These reports advise investors not only about individual companies, but also industry trends.

As you start identifying trends, you will also start understanding how your skills and abilities touch the people who are wrestling with these issues inside your target companies. Constantly ask yourself this fundamental question: When it comes to my boss or my boss's boss, the people who have the authority to hire me, what are they worried about? What are they thinking about? And how might someone with my background help?

Use these research principles to update yourself on the industry you've been working with most recently in your career. And you can ask these same questions to find entry points into new industries or companies that you'd like to consider for the next phase of your career. If you have even a passing interest in a new enterprise or industry, seek individuals who have some expertise in that particular profession or industry, and ask them what the key issues are. How are their issues different from the industry that you are coming from? How might your skills and experiences be transferrable to this new sector? Basically, you want general answers to the "How can I help?" question.

But don't try to help right away. You're still in a data-gathering role. But you're going to be tempted to say, "Aha! I know how to solve their problem (or help them achieve vision, business plan, and so forth). Ta da! Hire me, and I'll solve this." Don't go that far. Don't assume that's what the dialog is going to be about. Don't overstep. You'll have plenty of time later when you transition your HJM research meeting into an actual job interview.

Follow your curiosity, but trust you will have the chance to demonstrate your smarts and passion when the time is right (and if this profession/role/industry/company even still interests you). Your ongoing curiosity will make you a much better conversationalist in upcoming HJM research meetings and actual job interviews—provided, of course, that you continue to be interested in the career path you've been researching.

If you're losing interest, well, it may be disappointing, but it's better that you know now before you proceed any further down that line of inquiry. And waste any more time.

Remember, it's okay if your research *isn't* complete or even totally accurate or up-to-date. This may seem counterintuitive. Yes, you want to impress your HJM meeting partners and hiring managers with your understanding of your profession or industry. But you're not studying for an exam or writing a term paper.

For example, your TOP is a living document, a work in progress. It's subject to change, update, and correction.

Your purpose in the HJM research meetings is ultimately to get your meeting partners to help you fill in the blanks on your TOP and to open up to you about their business or expertise. If you come in like a know-it-all, ready to tell them what your proposed solutions are, you'll wreck your opportunity to make a valuable connection that could ultimately take you to your dream job. People like to help, and an incomplete TOP and questions confirming the trends and hot issues you have uncovered gives them a chance to contribute.

So, it's okay for you to not know everything—filling in the blanks and helping you understand will make your HJM research meetings that much more dynamic and engaging for both you and your meeting partner.

The important thing is for you to bring your research into your meetings, use it to ask intelligent questions and deepen your understanding of the path you have selected to explore.

The best thing you can do:
Ask quality questions based on research you do into the industries and organizations that interest you.

The worst thing you can do:
Try to fake it by just doing a cursory glance at Google hits and press releases.

The first thing you should do:
Ask yourself five new questions about a company or industry with every article, PowerPoint presentation, or analyst's report that you read.

Trendspotting with .ppt

Dale was exploring career possibilities and became interested in solar power. He knew from his old career that professional conferences were a great way to stay abreast of current issues. After conferences, PowerPoint presentations are frequently posted on the conference website. Since the topics of sessions often include "current trends" in the title and PowerPoint files always end in .ppt, he did a Google search on "solar power trends ppt." From this, he got conference presentations covering current issues, technologies, companies, and names of presenters. By going to conference websites, he was able to look for other related topics and expand his understanding of hot industry issues.

STEP 5

GET THE INTERVIEWS THAT COUNT AND RUN THEM LIKE A PRO

CHAPTER 20

It's Not Rude to Intrude

Think back on the days when you were employed. You had meetings all the time. They were an essential part of getting the job done. Granted, some of them were time-wasting hassles. But that was the fault of the people who ran the meetings, not the meetings themselves. Meetings are the modern market square where important business is conducted.

Whether you're between jobs or are busy with full-time work, meetings are equally essential for success. For managers, the only thing that will make them truly successful is their ability to meet and hire really great people. The smart ones know the value of meetings, even meetings when they don't have a specific need today. So, you're saving them a lot of time and trouble by coming to them first to propose a meeting. This way, they don't have to scurry around looking for you. You're doing people a professional favor by inviting them to sit down with you and explore ways that business can be done better. In this case, it's the business of you getting your next job. But who knows? It can also be the business of helping your meeting partners do their jobs better.

You're offering them a tool for their own core business issue—which is doing their job well (and, not insignificantly, growing their own careers). You're equipping these people with resources for their own success.

This is the attitude we want you to carry with you as you're gathering up the nerve to start asking for meetings. But we know that it might take a little doing to get your confidence and perspective up to this level. Maybe this is what your mind is telling you right now: These people are too busy to see someone like me.

Duncan's clients often say to him, "Why would they want to talk with me? I wouldn't want to talk with me." They're busy doing important work that's pulling down a paycheck. You're busy doing... what? Worrying about making those initial calls? The longer you're out of work, the larger the chasm seems to grow between you and the Great Employed.

Everyone is busy these days. And everyone's time is valuable, including yours. You're not imposing on their days, asking for favors. You're offering a business meeting during which real value will be exchanged. You know what the agenda is going to be, you're driving it, and you're going to stick to it. This could be the most productive meeting they'll have all week, even if you might be the main beneficiary of the encounter at the moment. They'll still have the satisfaction of knowing that their time was spent well helping someone else on his or her career journey.

You might be thinking that they're not going to want to see you because their company isn't hiring. Don't be so sure. Managers don't always advertise open positions. And even companies that have officially announced hiring freezes could be looking for additional help off the record. Never assume anything that blocks you from picking up the phone and making the initial meeting request. You just don't know what's going on behind closed doors until you get on the other side of them.

Two additional points to make here: The target company may not be hiring today, but it might be releasing some budget for positions in, say, three weeks. When that time rolls around, wouldn't it be better that you've already started relationships within the organization? That way, you have at least a three-week headstart on any candidates who might be competing with you for the job that you're perfect for. Any relationships you establish or nourish today will put you ahead of the competition tomorrow.

Also, you're not looking for a job with that company anyway. Remember? You're still in HJM research mode. So, it completely doesn't matter if that particular company has a hiring freeze that will endure through the next ice age. The person you want to talk with there knows someone who knows someone. Who knows someone.

Will this new attitude guarantee a successful appointment every time you ask for one? No. You'll still get blown off by a certain percentage of people who just don't get how important it is *to them* to take a meeting with you. These people don't understand that an essential key to their own success is the relationships they have outside of their own networking clusters. Too bad for them.

Say you have to endure five rejections for every five appointments that you do successfully land. Okay. Then, double the number of calls you make to hit your goal of having five to eight HJM research meetings a week, which will eventually lead you to your ideal job. Remember what IBM founder Thomas Watson said about the advantages of taking risks: "If you want to succeed, double your failure rate."

Is it worth the pain of small moments of rejection or embarrassment? When you think about the ultimate reward of landing the job that speaks to your abilities, motivation, and fit: You bet!

The best thing you can do:
Stay current on the issues, challenges, and new developments in your target industry and profession.

The worst thing you can do:
Spend your time being current on cable TV news, politics, and the gruesome "ain't it awful" crime of the week instead (unless, of course, your job is in media or politics).

The first thing you should do:
Set up a meeting with a recently retired executive. Get an executive's perspective on what is important in finding the right people and career success.

Just Pick Up the Phone and Call

Darrell decided it was time to switch careers, and he started looking for opportunities in marketing or product management. As his HJM networking progressed, one name kept coming up again and again: Bob Smith. Everyone told him the Bob Smith was the person he needed to know. Bob was not only the most connected product management guru in town, he was also a star. And none of Darrell's contacts felt they knew Bob well enough to arrange a direct introduction.

So, Darrell called Bob directly: "We haven't been introduced, but I have to tell you that I have spoken with three people whom I respect. They all know of you and have told me that for what I'm trying to do, you're the person I should talk to. Based on our mutual interests, it would probably be a good idea of us to meet."

Bob's response: "Well, sure! Three people mentioning my name? That's the best recommendation I could hope for."

True to his reputation, Bob introduced Darrell to four people *he* knew. And one of those referrals offered Darrell his new job.

CHAPTER 21

Get Past the Gatekeepers

If the very thought of picking up the phone and trying to sweet-talk your way past a gatekeeper makes you think about maybe starting that nap now, take some comfort in knowing that you're normal. In fact, the fear of the gatekeeper probably resides on a cellular level, connecting our modern DNA with those ancestors who faced down drawbridges and looked up just in time to see a vat of burning oil tipped just so right over their heads. (All they wanted was a job interview.)

Only now, what we worry about is the dreaded question, "May I tell him what this is in reference to?"

If you started your career in the 1970s or 1980s, you entered the work world when the gatekeeper was the administrative assistant (AA) to Mr. Big (MB). The economy was in the tank (sound familiar?). And the Baby Boomers were flooding the market, so there was no special need to be particularly nice to people who would call out of the blue asking for attention and a little bit of time. Nobody had ever heard of the War for Talent; eager workers were a dime a dozen. The job market was so hostile it felt as though AA and MB closed out their days laughing demonically while lighting cigars with flaming resumés.

The economy has swung between good and bad several times since then. And employers have cycled between freaking out over predicted labor shortages and assembling expensive severance packages. No one is feeling smug right now, most of all AAs, who belong to a rapidly disappearing profession. But still, you face the same challenge: To get to the person with the power to make a hiring decision, you have to get past the person with the power to let you in. Or keep you out.

In today's new world of getting through the doors, you have four different kinds of gatekeepers to contend with. This chapter shows you how to get past all four. Let's start with the most powerful of all gatekeepers: you.

1. **Gatekeeper: You.** It seems counterintuitive to think of yourself as the one who is standing squarely in the doorway between you and what could conceivably be your dream job. But, as long as you have other things to do (a nap? a piece of chocolate cake? Oprah?), you're keeping yourself on the outside of all the companies and contacts who can help you on your way.

   What you need is a plan beyond that little snippet of motivational genius—*just do it.*

   Have a script: But don't belabor it. Writing an excruciatingly pitch-perfect script could be another delay tactic.

   Have a schedule: You know when you sound your best. For you, maybe not first thing in the morning; it's amazing how the voice can broadcast that you're still in your pajamas. But if you are most comfortable breaking the ice with a voice mail message first, start the phone calls before your targets have come to work. (Word to wise: With call forwarding technology being what it is, your call may be forwarded to your target's mobile phone, which he just might answer— not happily if it's at 5 a.m.)

   Have a list: If you have a list of, say, 15 people you want to reach, you won't be sending out a lame or desperate vibe with each call. It's easier to keep your cool when you've got multiple chances at success.

   Have a seat: One of us (who shall remain nameless, let's just say that one initial is M) has the habit of pacing while deep in conversation on the phone—a kinesthete who thinks best while on the move. The resulting effect: A little freaky. A little wiggy. Definitely very breathy. Not very impressive.

The other one of us sounds calm, relaxed, grounded, in full command of the same conversation. Guess which one of us would get through to Mr. Big first. Answer: The one sitting down.

Have a businesslike attitude when you prepare to make your calls. You're not making personal calls. You're not even trying to sell anything. You're a professional peer hoping to make an appointment with another professional peer. To mutual advantage. That's it. Keep that in your head. And have a seat.

2. **Gatekeeper: The Administrative Assistant.** Not to be sexist or anything, but AAs are still mostly women, so we'll use the feminine pronoun for this section. Sorry, guys. Think about what it must be like to be her. She's in charge of the executive's calendar. She's tasked with making sure that not a split second of the busy executive's day is squandered by anyone who wants anything other than what's good for the company. And, if you're coming out of the blue, that could be you. Is it any wonder that she says to you, "Can I ask what this is in reference to?"

Be nice. But don't be schmoozy. Be brief, but don't be curt. Be real. If you and Mr. Big have a contact in common (especially if that contact was the one who connected the two of you), make sure the AA knows that you're coming courtesy of that recommendation. You're not dropping names. You're just letting her know that you've already been pre-approved.

Ask for her name. Why? Because she's a real human being who is doing you a favor. Not because you're implying a threat that if she doesn't come through you're going to tell on her. Don't use her name so often that you're sounding like you've just read a book on how to ingratiate yourself to the staff. Just use it real natural-like, as you would with anyone whose time, expertise, and access you deeply respect. You don't want to be manipulative and treat her like she's your oldest friend (*phony* alert). But, human nature being what it is, when we hear people call us by name we tend to lean in the direction of being friendly to them—at least at first.

The chances are good that the AA is going to tell you that the person you want to talk to is busy, on the phone, away, in a meeting, and so forth. And you'll get the choice of voicemail, leave a message with her, or email. She has just now become your consultant. Ask her what is the best way to get through to Mr. Big. Then, follow her advice. And say thank you before you hang up. Nicely. Admins have the power to influence opinions and schedules that extends beyond anyone's understanding—except for other admins, of course.

3. **Gatekeeper: Electronics.** You'll probably be given the option of voicemail or email. Martha, whose work requires her to call strangers all the time, prefers using both, starting with the voicemail. Her message (cheerful, friendly, organ-ized) starts with her name (obviously), immediately fol-lowed up by the phone number—spoken s-l-o-w-l-y This way, her target doesn't have to listen to the entire message all over again just to frantically copy down her phone num-ber before it flies away.

    She tells the person why she's calling, mentioning the name of their mutual acquaintance, if possible, and a brief syn-opsis of her larger agenda. Then, she says that she will be backing up the voicemail with an email. So the target knows to look for it and not to delete the message as possi-ble spam.

    After composing an email fully detailing what's on her mind, she concludes with the promise that she will call within a couple of days to make an official appointment for a conversation.

    Then, she calls when she promised to. If an unknown AA answers the phone, Martha has a response ready to the question, "Can I tell him what this is in reference to?" or

"And you're with…?" Her response: "He's expecting my call."

And she's in.

It's not a lie. And her friendly and confident tone of voice reassures the AA that she's not going to be serving a subpoena or trying to sell the boss a Player's Club membership.

4. **Gatekeeper: Mr. Big Himself.** Amazingly, these people often answer their own phones. Unfortunately, it's usually because they're thinking you're the scheduled conference call participant from Bangalore. So, don't be thrown by a disappointed—or peevish—voice on the other end. It's just the luck of the draw, that's all. You'll laugh about it over drinks during your second anniversary with the firm.

If you get Mr. Big Himself, and he's got the time to hear you out, lucky you! This is when you're going to find the information in Chapter 22, "What to Say After 'Hello,' " extremely handy.

The best thing you can do:
Remember, you are setting a business appointment. Just like you did when you had a job. People are busy. It was sometimes a challenge when you had the job—it just did not feel so personal then, and it shouldn't now.

The worst thing you can do:
Not try.

The first thing you should do:
Start. The first five are easy because you'll be calling people close to your own personal circle of contacts. The next ten are tougher. From then on, it will feel natural.

The Two-Week Blitz

John relocated his family to Southern California when his company transferred him three years ago after a reorganization. The new job was a promotion, but the constant organizational change was hard work and meant long hours. His wife and teenage children had a hard time settling into their new home, and they all missed their Midwestern lifestyle.

After his company was bought, John lost his job. This was a mixed blessing because it meant that the family could go back home again. So, John applied to job openings in his old hometown, but employers didn't want the expense of flying him out for interviews, not to mention the possible relocation expenses.

Frustrated by the long-distance search, John planned a two-week networking blitz to the area. He decided to line up as many HJM appointments as possible in the first week, with the idea of keeping the second week open and flexible for follow-up appointments and referrals. He then wrote a carefully crafted script to make it easy for his targets to agree to a meeting: "My wife and I grew up in the Midwest, and for the past three years, we have lived in Southern California. The sunshine is nice, but we are really ready to return to our Midwestern roots. I am going to be in town later this month and in your area talking to some other folks on Wednesday the 15th. Would you be willing to meet with me to help me get a read on the local market?"

John found that people were willing to meet because he was in the neighborhood and did not feel the pressure that they would have had if he were making a special trip to see them alone. By the end of the second week, he had conducted 28 meetings. Those 28 meetings turned into 3 formal job interviews and 2 offers, with relocation help included in both packages.

CHAPTER 22

What to Say After "Hello"

Want to feel really young again? Like, say, when you were in junior high? Here's what you do: Set aside a morning or afternoon to do nothing but call strangers and ask them for a date—well, in this case, an appointment for an HJM research meeting. You're staring at your call list, then at the phone, your call list, the phone. Suddenly, the prospects of being flat broke for the next three years seem preferable to the immediate almost-certainty of feeling like a 14-year-old doofus for the next three hours.

Maybe you just need some practice and a little helpful advice as to what to say after you say hello. We've put together a script based on suggestions that Duncan has used with his clients over the years. This isn't to put words in your mouth; we all know a phony script when we hear one, especially over the telephone. But it gives you a basic structure of what these opening conversations sound like when they're successful. And why they work.

As we get into the details, remember that your only objective is to get an appointment. Not to get a job and not to demand time right now to talk on the phone because you want information *now*. Weird, huh? You're a professional asking another professional for a business meeting. And you have every reason to expect that they'll at least be receptive to the idea. (Why not? As Jack Canfield has said: "Assume on your own behalf.") Here we go:

You: Hello Maryanne, this is (state your name). Sue Johnson thought that it would be a good investment of our time to meet. We had been talking about organizations in the area and my search for a new position in the industry. I was wondering if you were free sometime next week for no more than an hour to meet at your office. I would like to share a bit of my background and my goals, and then have you look at some research that I've done on the industry. And, of course, get some feedback from you. Sue thought you would definitely be a person to help me fill in some blanks. I want you to know that I'm not expecting you to know of any specific open positions. Although if you did, that would be great. My main objective here is just to fill you in on my objectives and get your perspective on what's happening in the industry to determine whether I'm on the right track as well as some ideas about who else would be good for me to connect with.

Let's dissect your little speech:

> *Sue Johnson*—You have a mutual contact; you're not some weirdo coming out of who knows where to make Maryanne's life a living hell.
>
> *a good investment of our time*—You're acknowledging time is valuable; that you two are peers; that there's benefit to meet for her as well (at the very least, she'd better be networking herself, but don't actually say that); and that you are only interested in booking a carefully considered appointment into your calendar, too. You wouldn't be reaching out to her if you hadn't already determined that this meeting has the potential of being good for business.
>
> *my search for a new position in the industry*—You're being upfront and authentic about looking for a job. Maryanne doesn't have to collude in any pretension that you're not.
>
> *for no more than an hour*—You've set a time limit. You have a specific plan, and you're not going to be camped in her office for a half day.
>
> *at your office*—Maryanne doesn't even have to look for her car keys or take a two-hour lunch.

research that I've done on the industry—You're coming into the meeting already equipped with knowledge and an informed perspective on where you want to be going in your career.

you would definitely be a person to help me fill in some blanks—You're coming into the meeting with a specific agenda and defined ways that she might actually be able to help out.

I'm not expecting you to know of any specific open positions. Although if you did, that would be great—Maryanne is reassured that she's off the hook regarding specific job opportunities. But you're also being real that this is what it's ultimately all about.

some ideas about who else would be good for me to connect with—Maryanne knows that you'll be happy with some additional introductions. And that it will be entirely up to her whether to share them with you.

What Happens If Maryanne Says Yes?

This is the only time in the entire book when we're going to tell you to play a little game. If there is anything even remotely related to a happy dance going on at your end of the line, don't let Maryanne know it. Play it cool, man, cool:

You: What about a time between 2 and 4 on Wednesday? Or alternatively, Friday morning between 9:30 and, say, 11? (Note the blocks of time and specific days. Don't make it the very next morning after the phone call. Keep your dignity.)

Maryanne: Hmm. I've already got appointments during those times.

You: What time would work for you?

Maryanne: (She gives you a time that you had already booked for doing... absolutely nothing.)

You: (Pause, pause) Yes. I can make that work. That will be great.

Then: *Get off the phone!* Duncan says that this is the crucial moment when all is going splendidly but then his clients feel compelled to say just one more thing. And it usually ends up being something really stupid. Like: "Really? Gee! I never thought you would say yes!" If you find yourself talking into the receiver even as you're putting it back in its cradle, you might want to think about your closing script.

If you have to say something else, conclude the conversation by double-checking date, time, and address. It's entirely possible that your head will be spinning with the residual nervousness of making the phone call in the first place, combined with the excitement of the success that you could totally screw up a small detail. And then miss the meeting altogether. So, calm down. Focus. Repeat the details and get Maryanne's confirmation.

End the conversation with, "I am looking forward to our meeting. Goodbye."

What Happens If Maryanne Says Maybe?

This is what *maybe* sounds like:

Maryanne: You know, I'm really busy right now, and I'm not really sure I can help you.

You: I really understand. People are often concerned about how they can be helpful. But I've found that once we start brainstorming, both of us end up pleased with the value of these meetings. I know everybody is busy these days. So, rest assured it will only take an hour—if that.

Maryanne: Well, tell me more about your background. What kind of job are you looking for?

You: For the last _____ years, I was _____,
which included everything from _____ to
_____. I'm exploring new ways that I can apply my
skills and background, particularly in the _____
industry (or profession). That's why Sue thought that it
would be good for both of us to meet. This would be a way
for both of us to share some market intelligence and I could
get your perspective on _____. Typically,
this takes no more than an hour and it is really helpful. I
thought meeting at your office would be most convenient for
you. Going out takes a huge chunk of time for people. (See
how we returned back to the meeting request? Patient and
thoughtful focus on the objective usually pays off.)

Maryanne: Send me your resumé and I'll see what I can do.

(Clearly, Maryanne hasn't read this book. She upped the
game a bit. So, you'll have to be a little patient with her. She's
going to be learning a lot by the way you handle this. Which
could come in very handy to her one day soon. And she's
going to want a meeting with *you*.)

You: Thank you for offering to look at my resumé. If you
know of a specific position you can help me with, that would
be great. Actually, one of the things I would like you to look
at is a profile of the type of opportunity I am looking for,
including some very specific industry information. I have
found it most helpful to take a portion of our time to share
that with folks and get their reaction. Later, if a resumé makes
sense, I'll be happy to share that with you. Again, if there is a
best time of day, I am certainly willing to work my schedule
around for you.

These are just suggestions on how you can be specifically effective in those "think fast on your feet" moments when you're trying to sound comfortable, friendly, and authentic in an
extremely unnatural moment. The first couple of times you try

this, it will be awkward. You will learn what wording works for you. Start with a script to keep you on track. Think about possible things people could say that might put you off track. Come up with a response that loops back to your request for a meeting. Take comfort in knowing that with practice you'll start easily filling up your calendar with great HJM research meetings.

You survived being 14. You'll survive this.

The best thing you can do:
Do it.

The worst thing you can do:
Don't do it.

The first thing you should do:
Give yourself permission to be awkward at first, if that's what it takes to get started. You will get better at this if you are thoughtful, genuine, and experiment a bit.

Preflight Checklist

Su-lin, a research scientist for the biotech industry, didn't especially enjoy networking—especially calling total strangers. But after a considerable amount of prodding and encouragement from an advisor, she picked up the phone and called the vice president of research for a fast-growing pharmaceutical company. To her amazement, he quickly agreed to a face-to-face meeting. They set a day and time to meet the following week, and she hung up the phone with a fresh surge of excitement and confidence.

On the day of their appointment, though, Su-lin discovered that she hadn't confirmed the company's location. No problem, she thought, she'll just look it up on the company's website. She jotted down the address, forgetting to also copy the vice president's direct-dial phone number. Once on the highway, she wished she had that phone number because traffic was backing up and it looked like she was going to be late now.

She arrived at the lobby within seconds of the appointment, feeling frazzled but grateful to be there. Now she could calm down, she thought. But the receptionist told her that the vice president worked at the new headquarters building, 6 miles across town. No, she didn't have his phone number; the company directory hadn't been updated.

By the time she finally got to the vice president's office, she was almost 30 minutes late. He certainly understood what had happened. But still, because of his crowded schedule, he could only give her a few minutes' time. Now completely off her game, Su-lin forgot to ask for his business card. And so, later, when she wrote a thank you note to him, she misspelled his name. That meeting was not destined to change her career, as she had hoped. But it did change the way she managed her networking. After that experience, she kept posted by her computer a checklist that she would follow during each phone call. She would not hang up until it was completed. On that checklist:

- ✓ Name
- ✓ Title
- ✓ Direct dial phone number
- ✓ Cell phone number
- ✓ Email address
- ✓ Address
- ✓ Date of appointment
- ✓ Time of appointment
- ✓ Address of appointment (if different from the contact's office address)

CHAPTER 23

Disrupt HJM Targets' Delay Tactics and Rejections

We know you're in a hurry to start making progress in your job search. But, let's face it, some people just aren't going to want to see you right away. By which we mean that some people know right away that they're just not going to want to see you. At all. (Yes, we know they're misguided.) But then others will definitely want to get together with you. Just not right now. Still others will need convincing.

How do you transform "no" into an appointment, even if it is a few weeks in the future? Practice preparation, perspective, and patience.

You remember what it was like when you were working full time and your calendar overflowed with competition for your time and attention. The idea of yet one more request for an hour of your day was probably too much for you to bear. So, you put things off until that distant day when perhaps your schedule might open up again. Did it? No. Not until you got laid off. Then it opened wide.

So, now you have all this time on your hands—time to brood and imagine all sorts of dread scenarios about your future. And now, delays feel like a very long time. A recently laid-off friend of Martha's, who happens to be an HR star, albeit an out-of-work one, confided to her that "Now that I know how it feels to wait for a promised phone call that never comes, I'm always going to keep my promises to call people who are looking for work." It seems strange that he would have to make that resolution now. But when you're busy, it's easy to lose track of time. When you're not busy, time just crawls. And minute by minute, the phone still doesn't ring.

When you reach out to a potential networking partner to request an HJM research meeting and you get a bit of a brush-off, don't take offense, be empathetic. They're busy; too busy to imagine what it might be like to be in your shoes one day. So, they need you to make it as easy for them to help you as possible:

"I really understand what you mean, everybody's really busy. Would it work better for me to come to you, so that you don't have to leave the office? That way, we make the best use of your time."

Or, they may tell you that they're too busy to talk to you right this very minute.

You might be disappointed that the earliest time when they can talk to you is three weeks away, when you really need a job *now*. But cast yourself forward three weeks from now. You'll have that appointment to look forward to (in addition to the other five to six appointments you'll have made for that week). And in the meantime, those intervening weeks will be filled with other appointments that you've been making all along. It's not like you'll be twiddling your thumbs for three weeks while you count down the days.

The other delay tactic you might experience will be, "I don't have any job openings." And that's one where you have to go back to your core script. "I honestly don't expect you to know of any job openings, but what I'm doing…" and just go right that to that basic script in which you reiterate your request for a meeting but that you're not expecting a job interview.

Don't be surprised if every once in a while you get this haughty message from one of your targets: "I don't do networking." The arrogance of that kind of rejection is almost laughable. If it wasn't so sad. You may be tempted to say, "Really? Well I'm going to remember you when you're looking for a job." But take the high road because that person *will* be remembering you when he's looking for a new job. And you'll want to show him how it's done.

Say: "Yeah, I know what you mean. Networking can really be a pretty lame affair. And so, what I can tell you is that I'm very conscientious about making sure the meetings are an excellent investment of time for both of us. There's a lot to be learned, even though there aren't specific opportunities that you might know of. I've been amazed at how often these connections have made huge difference. And I've been able to help them in the future, too."

Or use the *feel-felt-found* approach to deal with that ridiculous response to your request: "You know, I felt exactly the same way as you did when I was vice president of such-and-such. But then, I realized that I was missing two things: One was an opportunity to meet really great and talented people, and the other one was the opportunity to build my connections. Fortunately, I realized that in time to do something about it. Because now that I'm in transition, it's not such a pain in the neck to get reconnected back in the community."

That's a mouthful, to be sure, but what makes that response a success is that you are speaking to your target as a peer, not as a pitiful, poor networker who has to slap on a brave smile before leaving the house in the morning.

If you still get stiff-armed by targets who say they don't have time to meet with anyone just now, it might be helpful to remind them that these meetings are as important for them as they are for you: "Really? You know, as a manager, I always found that the most important thing that contributed to my success was meeting and hiring really great people. And frankly, I wouldn't ask for your time if I didn't think it was worthwhile for both of us."

Prepare yourself for all the *no's, maybes,* and *laters* you can think of. Imagine all the different kinds of rejections that might get under your skin a little bit. And have a prepared, rehearsed answer for each one of them.

The best thing you can do:
Think of this as a sport and keep score. This is a skill, and with time, you get better at it. And like all sports, some plays work sometimes, but not other times.

The worst thing you can do:
Run out of lists of people to call. You don't want to be in the position of having to fill the funnel from scratch again, just when you might be feeling the most discouraged.

The first thing you should do:
Imagine every kind of response that could make you feel rejected or put down. Prepare a script for each of these responses. Compare your responses with others who are in the search.

Telephone Tag Winner!

John was frustrated. For three weeks, he was trying to connect with Ed, who worked at the local wireless communications company. He had heard that a new product was about to be launched and thought the company would be looking for a major account salesperson to promote the product. After the first three attempts, he got one return call from Ed, which he missed. He called back twice again, but got voicemail each time. The next time John called, Ed answered the phone. John started his request for a meeting, but Ed interrupted, "Look, John, I am in a meeting now and I know you have been trying to reach me. But this week is really a bad week for us to talk. Can you call next week?"

John groaned inwardly at the idea of waiting another week. But what was worse was hanging up now without having made any progress at all. So, John took a chance at being just a little pushy: "Ed, I know you are really busy and I appreciate your willingness to meet with me. Trading calls is time-consuming for both of us. If you have your calendar in front of you, let's take a quick moment and set a time to meet. I will do a confirmation email. Then, we can cross this off of our to-do list." Ed agreed, and they set an appointment for the next week right then and there. Three weeks later, John joined the company as the western area new accounts manager. Ed later told him, "I appreciated your persistence. It was professional and respectful of my time."

CHAPTER 24

Own the Agenda to Make Every Minute Count

Notice, first of all, that the title of this chapter is not "How to Ace the HJM Research Meeting." There's a very good reason for this. Unlike the conventional job interview (where it is your job to ace it), your primary objective is not to sit passively in the chair coming up with snappy answers to interview questions. Your job is to exchange information with a professional peer. (Even if that person holds a spot that's higher on the org chart than your last job, you're peers right now.) Sure, it's best if the two of you "click" and an enduring business networking relationship is born. But you can still get a lot out of the meeting even if that is the first and last time the two of you ever see each other.

Unlike the conventional job interview, your mission here isn't to snag a job offer. It's to come away a little wiser, a little sharper, a little more informed than you were an hour before. You'll have at least one new introduction to follow up on (preferably three, five, or even more). You'll have deeper understanding about how to come closer to your ideal job. And it really is just fine that the person you're meeting with doesn't leap for joy and shout, "Where have you *been?* We've been looking for you for years!" Then, they show you to the corner office that they kept vacant in the faith that you would come along one day.

The core difference between the HJM research meeting and a conventional job interview is that with HJM research meetings *you're* the one in charge. You called the meeting, and so you own the agenda. In fact, you're the one asking the questions. Unless your meeting partner has read this book (which would be nice, but we can't have everything), he is probably going to be a little uncertain about exactly what you have in mind for the hour. And so, it's up to you to lay out the plan and then control it from "hello" to "thanks so much for your time and ideas."

Here's what the agenda looks like:

Five minutes early: Be There. Don't get lost.

We don't need to expand on that, do we? Didn't think so.

First five minutes of the meeting: Positioning Phase.

After basic, and very brief, icebreaking chitchat, get started by giving a brief run-through of the agenda. This way, your partner knows what's in store for the hour and can settle in, no longer distracted by the question of "Okay, where is this leading?" This is also the time when you reiterate that you're indeed in the market for a job, but it's absolutely nonessential for him to know of any openings for this meeting to be a good investment of time for both of you. Here's what you say:

"I want to tell you just a little bit about my background, share with you some of what I'm targeting in my objectives and the research that I've done on some of the organizations that I'm interested in. And I'd like you to take a look at what I've done and get your feedback on it. Maybe you have some specific suggestions and ideas. I'd also like to talk to you about the trends that are going on in the industry and the implications that they might have on my search. And then, if you have some suggestions on where to go from here, I'd very much like to talk about that as well."

Use the last two minutes of the Positioning Phase to tell your two-minute story (see Chapter 25, "Get Their Attention: Tell Your Story in Two Minutes Flat"). This is a brief description of your career history and what brings you to this meeting today. Conclude your discussion with your search objectives and what you want to achieve next in your career.

Next 10 minutes: Stimulus Phase.

This is where you bring out your targeted opportunity profile (TOP) and lay it on his desk. Walk him through the upper part of the profile, pointing out the kinds of opportunities that you are looking for and the kind of people who might hire you. Show him the associations that you have identified and quickly look through the list of companies that might hire you.

After you walk him through the TOP document, sit back and simply ask, "So, what do you think? Can you tell me about any of the organizations on the list? Or do you know anyone who might be in charge of someone in my target position?"

This is when they can scan through your list and give you a lot of information, names, email addresses, and phone numbers to fill in your blanks. Offer to let them mark it up to their heart's content. You know you have them excited about your journey when they pull out their pen and start writing all over it. This is a good thing.

Don't be thrown if they suddenly set the TOP aside and start asking you more pointed questions about your goals and ambitions. You may have just slid into an actual job interview. That could also be a good thing.

Next 40 minutes: Information Exchange Phase.

Use this time to start asking for information about the industry, techniques, trends, professional practices, unmet needs or frustrations prevalent in the profession or your targeted geographic location. Ask questions that begin with "I've noticed...." For example, "I've noticed that one of the trends in the industry is a real shift in buyer behavior. What's your observation about how companies are responding to this change? What needs are you noticing going unmet?"

This is also the time to ask if they know of anyone who has made the journey that you are on. You want to know the key drivers to success for the role you're targeting, what takes a person to that 20% star factor. What are the true hiring criteria for this role? It's not minimum qualifications that you're asking about. You want to know what the performance criteria is that takes a person in your targeted role to the top of their class.

If you are changing career paths, this is your opportunity to mine for examples and stories of people who are exceptions to the typical step-by-step career path for your targeted profession. Ask the question, "Have you ever known anyone to transition careers in this way? How did they pull it off? Who should I talk to? Did you do it? What were your lessons along the way?"

Final 5 minutes: Wrap It Up and Get Gone.

Remember, you're still in the charge of the meeting. And so, you want to leave yourself plenty of time to exit gracefully, well before your meeting partner starts shuffling in his chair and you can see an "isn't it about that time?" thought balloon above his head. Leaving on a clumsy, rushed note could destroy all the impressive progress that you made in the previous 55 minutes.

Your goals for your last five minutes are simply these: Quickly review the actions that you both have agreed to take and ask your partner how he wants to be kept in the loop as you move ahead on the introductions and suggestions you received in the meeting. Be sure to then thank him for his time.

Should the meeting go long and you're not feeling impatience fill the room, just stop for a moment (preferably no later than the 55-minute mark) and say, "I made a commitment to you that this would be only an hour meeting. But it now looks like we're going long. Is this okay with you? Or should we make another appointment to continue the conversation?" It's considerate. It's practical. And it definitely protects you from bumping into the next appointment in the doorway or leaving with the feeling that they couldn't wait to get you out of there.

The minute you are at your computer, send your meeting partner an email thanking him for his time and promising to follow up as you progress.

That's it. One hour that could change your life.

The best thing you can do:
Recognize that these meetings are yours to run. This alone gives you a position of strength that no job interview scenario can provide.

The worst thing you can do:
Give into temptation or desperation and blurt out, "Do you think there's a job for me in this company?"

The first thing you should do:
For each meeting, write down the agenda with specific questions you want to ask. Refer to the agenda throughout the meeting to make sure you don't miss anything and that you're keeping yourself on track.

You Never Know Where One Question Will Take You

When Jonathan lined up an HJM research meeting with the president of a computer peripherals company, he noticed that the president seemed surprisingly eager to meet with him. Picking up on a cue that this meeting might morph into a real job interview, Jonathan said on a whim, "Is there anyone else you think I should meet with while I'm visiting your office?" As a result of that one inspired question, his single meeting with the president transformed into a full day of interviews with the chief financial officer, the vice president of sales, and a business unit leader.

Taking advantage of this lineup of one-on-one meetings, Jonathan asked each of these people, "When you look at how the sales operation is working today, what do you think could be done differently? What could make a difference in the revenue? What could be improved?"

These questions gave the CFO and the business unit manager a rare opportunity to fully discuss their frustrations with the way one business unit was performing. These insights equipped Jonathan with some extremely valuable ideas on how he could help the company pursue market opportunities that were being overlooked. While he didn't "give away the store," in his follow-up discussions with the president and the vice president of sales, he definitely demonstrated that he grasped the challenges the company was facing. And that he already had specific solutions in mind for them.

Those solutions made him irresistible. They offered him a job—one that was also irresistible.

CHAPTER 25

Get Their Attention: Tell Your Story in Two Minutes Flat

"So. Tell me about yourself."

In the HJM research meeting, your main role is to ask questions and listen. But you are going to have to tell your meeting partner who you are and why you're looking for a new job. Without a structure to help you build your background in a positive light—and within a short amount of time—you run the risk of ending on a down note (especially if you've been laid off) or rambling or taking up the entire meeting talking about yourself or being just plain boring.

This two-minute structure keeps your presentation contained and rolling along toward a positive conclusion that highlights who you are, how you've grown, and what you want to do next. It then sets you up to remain in control of the rest of the meeting, so you don't find yourself thrown into traditional job interview format where you've lost control and now you're the one fielding questions. The two-minute story structure is so essential to any job search campaign, as it really serves as the foundation of any powerful discussion about what you do and what your potential is as an employee for an organization. Its potential is grounded in the story of your career, which really reveals, based on your past experience, your ability, your motivators, and your fit to a team. It's about what you know, what makes you tick, in other words your motivation, and a little bit about your personality and style, particularly as it relates to how you fit in.

A really well-disciplined story fundamentally makes or breaks the HJM meeting (or even a conventional job interview, for that matter). So you want to write it out and rehearse it. You want to try it on people you know. You want to make sure it's clear. And that it gives people a vivid picture of what you did and who you are and how that ties to where you're going today.

You want to get good at it well in advance of telling it during an HJM meeting. (A reason why you shouldn't get discouraged if your target puts you off by a few weeks.) You want to get so good at it that when you're doing it, it feels relaxed and conversational even though you've heard it yourself 100 times.

There are six sections to this two-minute story. Section 1 is your opening positioning statement. Section 2 is your education and early career basics. Section 3 is a series of positions that you've held, what you learned and discovered about yourself along each phase of your career. Section 4 is the motivation of why you went to the next step and how it always represented forward progress.

Section 5 is finally skipping through what your current situation is to what your objective is. You touch on the situation but you really focus on the closing statement about your objectives. And Section 6 is a closing phase, which would be a question, but one that keeps you in control of the conversation.

Here's an example of how it goes and why each element serves you.

Section 1: Opening Positioning Statement
"Throughout my career, I've always been interested in operations and how to improve the numbers through improvement of both people and processes. My dad told me I should learn accounting, 'the language of businesses,' he called it."

Section 2: Education
"So I got my degree in accounting…."

Section 3: Experience

"… and joined an aerospace company as a financial analyst. The company made nacelles. It's that housing you see that wraps around engines on the airplanes."

Who cares about (or has even heard the term) nacelles? A lot of people do, but probably not your meeting partner. Still, by being specific in this way, you're grounding the story in the context of something that people can identify with. Give people pictures that they can relate to, an "Aha" moment that allows them to connect what you do with something they recognize from their own experience. If you stay too much in the realm of professional jargon, you may lose your partner's attention. Don't linger, though. Keep your conversation moving.

"It was there that I learned the foundations of cost accounting and analysis in a very complex and technical manufacturing environment."

Now, this is one sentence and it solves the problem of people with long careers where they may have had four or five different positions in one company. You don't need to run through a laundry list of titles and responsibilities, like, "I did this and I did this and I did this." You only need to talk about foundations. And skip details that don't count.

Section 4: Progress in Your Career

Moving on: "I was asked by my boss to be part of a series of projects to implement a new IT system as well as a number of initiatives in support of ISO-9000."

This sentence is structured to show that *others* thought you were good. It also reveals the depth of your job knowledge.

Your story goes on: "It was there that I learned about project management and the nuances of processes and people."

What you're really saying here is "I work well with people and I get it."

This whole section toggles back and forth between "I did this and I learned this," "I did this and I learned this." With each progression, you show how people noticed your performance and gave you increasingly important assignments. Also, with each progression, the level of importance of the people noticing you is also increasing. Phrases such as "this turned out well" imply that you made it turn out well.

"I also really enjoyed not just the deal making but getting a broader view of a competitive landscape."

You're throwing in motivation and perspective. So, it's what you enjoy doing, what engages you.

"About this time, the commercial aircraft industry was in a downturn and several executives left the company and started a new business in irrigation." There are always times in people's careers when there are unexpected turns that represent opportunities or challenges. And it's important if you can to talk about how you adapt to that. "They asked me to join them and I at first thought it was too low-tech."

Whenever you think you've got a cue on what could be a negative or an objection, you can send a very subtle message that "I agree with what you're saying." It's a little bit of a *feel-felt-found* approach. It's also a way of demonstrating that you have personal history in being willing to keep your mind open.

"The smaller company allowed me to work directly with strategic planning as a director, then VP for the company."

Every step, even to smaller companies, is an advancement. And so even if you end up at the same job level, but you went into a smaller company, your scope of responsibility might have expanded. Or now you have the chance to work with real strategy, or you got to work closer with really important people.

Always describe your next steps as advancements—advancements in position, learning, and experience.

Section 5: Briefly Addressing Your Current Situation

"This included an initiative to offshore some of our manufacturing…" (notice the contemporary issue, another new thing that you learned) "…where we were bought and I was packaged out."

Section 6: Moving On to Your Current Objectives and Concluding with a Question

"And what I would like to do is to transfer my operations background in technically demanding, high-volume products to the medical device industry."

Here, you're establishing a goal that does not end on a down note of being out of a job. Then, you follow this with a question that's based on research, demonstrating that you've done your homework and you have given this some thought.

"It strikes me that in the medical device industry there are many parallels to the kind of work I've done in the past. But I'm very interested in what your perspective is."

Interviewers will often focus on the very last thing that you said. So if the last thing you said is that you're out of work and looking for a job, that's what they'll focus on. But if the last thing you said is what you want to do and that you're interested in their perspective on that, they'll react to that and actually go back deeper into your story.

All of this can and should be delivered in two minutes.

Keep it short. Remember, you're not there to talk about yourself. You're there to gather more data and perhaps move your job search forward with additional names, contact information, and ideas. Still your HJM research meeting partner is going to want to know about you so that he can put into context who you are, who you say you are, and what your next best steps might be. Tomorrow, next week, and well into your career.

While the two-minute story might take some extra effort to refine and rehearse to the point where you don't sound rehearsed, the effort will pay off big in the end.

The best thing you can do:
Think about how you can best tell your career story in highlights.

The worst thing you can do:
Turn your two-minute story into an oral resumé, filled with dates and the phrase, "and then... and then... and then."

The first thing you should do:
Make a list of all the times you advanced because someone noticed how great you are at what you do.

From Sawdust to Civil Engineering

Mark had some college, dropped out, and became a logger. He loved the outdoors, but after an injury, decided to return to college and get a degree in civil engineering.

Now in his late 30s, with no professional experience, he felt he was at a disadvantage competing with younger college grads and those with more civil engineering experience. He also thought that his work as a logger was of no relevance to life as a professional civil engineer.

In his HJM interviews, he began to ask more detailed questions about the daily experience and essential skills of experienced civil engineers in the field. He learned that engineers leading projects were responsible for managing contractors and labor working with heavy equipment. They frequently had to deal with issues at the worksite not foreseen during design and contracting phases of a project. He also learned that newly minted college students often lacked credibility with labor and contractors and had limited knowledge about heavy equipment and safety issues.

As he refined his two-minute introduction, he included his work as a logging supervisor, his success managing men and equipment in difficult terrain, as well as the fact his team never had a serious injury. This distinction proved to be the reason he was selected for the job ahead of other applicants.

CHAPTER 26

Flipping the HJM Meeting into a Job Interview

Don't worry. We haven't lost sight of the fact that it's a *job* you're looking for, not the "fun" of filling out your targeted opportunity profile (TOP) through a vast and varied collection of hidden job market (HJM) research meetings. We know: It stops getting fun really fast as you fill up your car yet again for yet another HJM research meeting, and you're wondering exactly when one of these meetings is going to bring you in front of someone who actually has the power to hire you—for the role that you want to be hired for.

You're about to be rewarded for your patience. This chapter is about what to do when you finally meet someone who might ultimately say, "When can you start?" But first, let's do a quick refresher on the steps that have brought you to this great opportunity.

You started your HJM research meeting process with the understanding that really great networking extends beyond the people you personally know (the first degree) and even the people that they know (the second degree). We've warned you against using your first-degree contacts as mere messengers you ask to pass your resumé on to their contacts. And you've been personally following up on all introductions, expanding your circles of contacts and busting out of clusters as you go. You've left your resumé at home each time (right?); you've brought your TOP document with you each time (right?). And, even though it might take you more than just a few degrees of connection to finally meet the person who has the ability to hire you for a job that you'd actually want, you've begun to appreciate how this networking system is working for you—and will continue working for you even after you've happily landed in your new job.

With each meeting, you are clear that you're looking for a job. But you're also clear that you don't expect that person to have or know of any particular opportunity. You've remained sincerely and authentically in research mode, learning to enjoy these conversations even more as you go. Then one day, you find yourself sitting in front of the person who has the power to change your life—or at least has the potential to offer you the job that you've been holding out for.

But at this point, you may be the only one who realizes it. In the hidden job market, you could be coming into these conversations well before your meeting partner has given any thought to actually solving a problem or meeting a need by hiring someone new (read: you).

Listen for what sales professionals call *buying signals*. That's your cue to the possibility that she's beginning to think of you with more specific business interest in mind. And that's when you can start subtly transforming the HJM research meeting into an actual job interview. But you still have to do it in such a way that you stay true to your original agenda of just data gathering.

Above all, enjoy the meeting as a *conversation*. It's still not a conventional job interview. You are in a meeting of peers. You're not on the spot to "ace" the meeting.

Uncovering Hidden Needs and Wants

In the hidden job market research meetings, we always have to be attuned to what needs your meeting partner has that could drive the decision to hire someone *just like you*. And these needs are typically hidden—at least at first. Because you're not on a job interview, they may not be readily discussed. Or they're hidden because they may not have been completely formulated in the mind of your meeting partner. Or these needs might be considered a competitive secret. It's still up to you to find out what those hidden needs are and understand how you might be the one to help solve their problem.

You do this through conversation. It's give and take between two peers equally interested in the topic of discussion. This is your chance to see the world through your potential hiring manager's eyes. And the way you do that is to invite her to share her perspective. Here's an example of what such a conversation might look like:

> "You know, I was reading the other day that professional service firms have to do a much better job in demonstrating how their services produce better financial results. Do you think that's true?" Your meeting partner is bound to say yes to that. And so then you might follow up with, "How is that trend affecting how you sell and deliver services?"

Have follow-up questions prepared: "When you choose people to be on your team, what characteristics do you think are important?" With this type of question you're transitioning from the problem overall to the solution—what the meeting partner sees as the essential characteristics of the top 20% performers for dealing with that problem. From that series of questions alone, you'll be surprised what you learn about her hiring criteria.

Another example of this is, "You know, I've noticed a number of retailers are moving to smaller urban-based outlets to combat the big-box retailers. We did something like this in our western region and had some interesting results. That seems like a promising strategy, but what's your perspective?" This is an example of where you give a hint about something you've done.

The idea here is to elicit a *conversation*, not start a question-and-answer volleyball game. That's deadening and will not ignite an inspired conversation. Still, you will have to serve up the first question to get the conversation started. Not everyone is a talented conversationalist. So, if you want some models of how it's done, stay away from the entertainment-oriented talk shows (otherwise, you might come off as a Las Vegas lounge act in an attempt to be funny). Instead, watch Larry King or Charlie Rose, or Oprah, to study how their thoughtful questioning gets the conversational ball rolling with their guests.

You're not the only one who might be wrestling with shyness. You can be sure that more than one of your meeting partners might also be a little worried about how the meeting will turn out. If your meeting partner is a bit shy or reticent, you will probably have to work a little harder to get the conversation off the ground. Try the reporter's trick of loading your question with a false or slightly controversial assumption. That will give your meeting partner something exciting to dig into, losing self-consciousness in the process (you hope). Here's an example:

> "In my research, I've been coming across a frequently expressed opinion that to be successful in western region sales you have to have been born and raised in the West. I have a hard time believing that. What do you think?" (Notice that you're taking pains not to align yourself with the false assumption yourself; but if the context of your question is at least a little controversial, it might inspire your partner to open up more around the subject.)

This is an excellent way of opening up new avenues in your conversation and demonstrating that you're keeping up with what's happening in your industry or profession. But use this technique carefully. You want to provoke conversation (especially if it's stalled). But you don't want to provoke your meeting partner. If your meeting partner is feeling oddly peeved by your visit, she could remember that feeling as having been peeved at you.

Finally, be careful that your conversation about hidden wants and needs doesn't turn into a brainstorming session about possible solutions. You may feel compelled to show your meeting partner what you're capable of—and how nimbly your mind works. But you're not there to provide free consulting. Regardless of how brilliantly you come up with new ideas, they might not be so "new" to your target company. And you could risk facing down a daisy chain of responses: "tried that; did that; won't work; tried that; did that; won't work." And if you do happen to get caught up in the challenge of problem solving, you could conceivably overrun your allotted hour's time—and perhaps feel exhausted, rejected, and used. And foolish.

Martha calls that feeling the "dancing bear syndrome." The minute you start feeling like a dancing bear, you know you've lost control of your own power and are now on the performing end of someone else's short leash.

If you start going down a brainstorming path, stop and say, "You know, it sounds like this is something we really want to talk about in a lot more detail. This is an area that I'm really interested in, but I don't want to be presumptuous. I would want to learn a lot more about how it works here, and what would be the best solution for you."

It could be, however, that if your meeting partner starts asking what you would recommend as solutions to a particular problem, you may have just spotted your first buying signal.

Spotting Buying Signals

So, how do you spot the signs that the research meeting might be transforming into a job interview? The trick is knowing the difference between your own wishful thinking and a true buying signal. Here are some examples of what might be buying signals:

- Your HJM meeting partner quickly glances at your TOP, sets it aside, and starts asking more detailed questions about your background.
- She wants you to meet other people within the organization.
- She starts selling *you* on the advantages of working for her company.
- She starts talking about a particular problem the company is trying to solve or an opportunity it's trying to win.
- She starts posing hypothetical questions to you, "What would you do in a situation like...?"
- She starts coming up with specific reasons why you probably wouldn't be a good fit. This could be a buying signal in disguise. She's already imagining you inside the company, and each objection is an invitation for you to address the problem and position yourself as a good fit for the role, company, or culture after all.
- She asks you how you would feel about a lower-ranking job title. It's not always a bad idea to take a job with a lower-ranking role, even though it might appear to be a demotion on your job history. In the past ten years, the trend was to inflate job titles to be attractive as employers in a labor-shortage environment. Now that we're in the opposite employment climate, there will be some correction in the number of, say, vice presidents, inside a company.
- She asks you whom among the competition you have already spoken to. This could be a buying signal. (Human nature drives us to want what the other guy has, right?) But it could also be a cheap maneuver to see whether you might spill any competitive secrets. This is the time for you to demonstrate how discreet you can be.
- She says, "Hold on a minute, I want to send an email to somebody." (We're assuming here that she's *not* just emailing her lunch date to say "I might be a little late because this windbag won't leave my office.")

- She asks you, "What does your schedule look like next week?"
- She mentions in the *middle of the meeting* that you should fill out an application. (If that suggestion happens at the beginning of the meeting, reiterate that you're there to discuss the industry and some ideas that you have for your job hunt, and you did not expect there was an opening. But then ask, "Is there something specific you were thinking about?")
- She starts to explain the hiring process, perhaps even interrupting the meeting to send you to Human Resources. That completely derails the HJM culture of the meeting, but you might as well go with it. Great jobs have been landed this way.
- She asks you how soon can you start. Uh, buying signal.

If your meeting partner starts getting very interested in the prospects of having you aboard, you're going to see many variations of these buying signals. How you handle them will keep you in control of moving the meeting toward a job offer. (Even if the meeting transforms into an actual job interview, you are always the one in ultimate control. Remember that.)

Gently lead your meeting partner to the realization that there is a role for you in the company. If you're meeting this person through your HJM networking process, you may be coming in well in advance of a real job opening or even an actual need being identified within the company. So, the buying signals that you're observing could be completely subconscious for your meeting partner. Some gently worded questions could bring your partner to her own eureka moment: You are just the person they'd been looking for all along. Only they didn't realize it... until now.

> "Based on our conversation up to this point, it sounds like you're thinking about a specific situation. Can you say more about that?" (Here, you're allowing your meeting

partner to give you all the details of what the role might be and why it will be important to her to have that role filled by someone like you. You're actually giving her the chance to sell herself on the idea of bringing you onboard—while you're just sitting back, listening very carefully. And taking excellent notes.)

"So how soon do you want to have somebody in place to work on that issue?" (Here, you're inviting your meeting partner to begin imagining that she could have someone actually working on the problem by a specific day.)

"It sounds really intriguing to me. What else would you want this person to do?" (Here, you're zeroing in on the components of the job description that could be a great custom fit for you.)

Another question you might ask is, "This position that I'm describing in terms of my targeted opportunity profile, is that the kind of position that you hire for or you might hire for?"

In response to her suggestion that you speak with a colleague: "Why is it important for us to meet? What do they do?" You're just trying to understand where they fit in to the big picture; don't give the impression that you're deciding whether meeting additional people is worth your time. Of course it is.

And now for the closing question:

"You know, I'm really interested in this kind of a role within your organization. What would be the next steps? Where shall we go from here?"

With that simple question, you're putting both of you squarely on the path to an actual job offer. This transitional conversation you just had probably won't be the last interview on your way to a job offer from this company. But it is definitely the essential first step toward that destination.

You have kept your dignity but reemphasized your increasing interest in exploring more specific opportunities with the company.

Go for it. You've earned it.

The best thing you can do:
Keep in mind that any one of these HJM research meetings might transform into a job interview at any moment.

The worst thing you can do:
Expect that you can turn every HJM research meeting into a job interview.

The first thing you should do:
Work on your conversation skills by observing the masters at their craft.

The Real Value of Knowledge

Although Matt was originally trained as an engineer, he spent a decade working for a Fortune 100 computer company on solving manufacturing problems. That was his real passion. Unfortunately, Matt lost his job when his company moved all its manufacturing operations overseas.

At first, he thought this could be his chance to do something radically different with his life. So he went to cooking school, with the idea of perhaps becoming a chef. As much as he loved cooking, however, he found that he couldn't tolerate a chef's working hours. So he decided to reserve cooking for a pleasurable pastime. And he returned to the drawing board.

Through connections, he discovered a small company that manufactured precision screws and fasteners for nuclear reactors and spacecraft. These were one-off items to be manufactured to exquisite specifications from supremely expensive material. The slightest error meant that the item must be discarded—posing an intolerable expense in wasted materials and time.

In a conversation with one of the managers, Matt discovered that the company was struggling with the problem of how to reduce that waste. And he casually began to suggest ideas that were common and accepted practices in his former company. But these solutions were revelations to the small company. So the executives invited him to accept the position of director of quality.

Matt was astonished to discover that this knowledge that he had taken for granted could make such a profound and valuable difference to this smaller company.

STEP 6

NEGOTIATE EVERYTHING

CHAPTER 27

How to Nudge a Dud

Here's the situation: You've had a series of really successful HJM research meetings, and a few of them have even transformed into almost-formal job interviews. One company has invited you to come back to meet additional team members and decision makers. And each conversation has led to an increased level of excitement about the possibility of you being part of the organization. You can just feel that an offer is on its way to you any day now. Any day... any day... any day. And then! Nothing.

Somebody got distracted on the company's end and allowed the conversation to disappear through a wormhole. Lost and gone forever. (At least that's how it seems.) It's disappointing when it happens once. It's really disheartening after it's happened several times. Clearly, you discover, you have to take control over this phase of the process, too. But how do you do that without coming off as pushy, manipulative, speedy, or needy?

First: Have more than one iron in the fire. This will take care of the neediness and the nerves. Remember that funnel? Even if you have three to five "favorite" possibilities out there, don't stop maintaining your funnel. Make sure your calendar is still full of HJM research appointments, and that you still have a long list of people you have yet to call. You can always gracefully stop the process after you have said yes to the perfect job offer (still with a couple in backup mode, just in case something falls through). But just knowing that the process is still in full swing will help you avoid that squeaky neediness that sounds in your voice even though you're trying your best to at least look nonchalant.

With your head in good shape, you can confidently stay in the driver's seat of the interviews all the way up to the actual job offers themselves. (Notice we used the plural form; your goal is to have multiple offers in play at once.)

Next: If you strongly believe that a job with a particular company is an attractive possibility—and you're thinking that the hiring manager might agree with you—try to bring the hiring manager up to speed with your agenda by asking questions that plant the idea in her mind. And position the discussion against the backdrop of timing (even a sense of urgency—but an urgency based on her ideal scenario, not on your pressing need to scare up next month's rent):

> "If you're looking at bringing a person like me into this opportunity (project, company), how soon would you like that person to start? What's your sense of timing around this?"

Or

> "It seems you are really interested in seeing results in the role we are talking about. How soon would you need to get started to allow a ramp up for a new person and see the returns realized on time?" You might have just helped her realize, "Oh my gosh! Right away!"

Or even, a bolder

> "Who would need to approve a budget for this position?"

Then, ask whether anyone else should be consulted before a decision is made. "Yes? Okay, should we arrange that meeting now, while I'm still here?" Once you leave the building, you may lose the hiring manager's focus and attention. And that appointment might never be made. Next stop: Wormhole City.

The worst-case scenario here is that the hiring manager will candidly tell you that there's no rush on this position. And, perhaps, the company is very truly saturated with one nasty hiring freeze. Okay, fair enough, at least you know. But that hiring freeze could be lifted at any time—especially if the hiring manager discovers that you might get away from them. In that case, a sudden surplus may arise in the budget that just fits an attractive compensation package for you.

That's why it's important to always stand on gracious ground, even when the hiring manager regretfully says to you, "We're sorry, it's not a good time for us."

To which you say, "I completely understand. I'd like to keep the lines of communication open, if you would like that as well. Even if the timing isn't right, right now. Who knows, maybe in the future." That future could be only a matter of a few weeks away.

What if you know the company needs your services desperately right now? And you need income right now. Do you offer your services as a consultant in the meantime? You could, but as with all stop-gap measures, this one comes with a hefty liability. If you really want to be fully employed by a single company, and you don't want to be a consultant, by offering your services as a consultant first, you could be sending the company confusing signals. If the company already has access to your services, without the commitment of a full-time job, your hiring manager might not be so motivated to bring you on full time. Additionally, if you're solidly booked working for this company as a consultant, you've taken yourself off the market for finding and landing that job you really want. So, by the time you reenter the hidden job market, you will have set yourself back several months.

As unnatural as this may sound, ultimately you're the one who will put the brakes on the forward movement of any job offer. It might be the perfect offer and you may want to leap at it. But graciously ask for a few days to consider the offer. (Don't say, "I'd like time to think about it." That sounds gamey and reluctant. In this economy, you don't want to sound like you're a tease just because you got the idea somewhere that "I'll think about it" makes you all the more attractive by playing hard to get.)

Simply say: "This is wonderful. And I'm really interested in this opportunity. But I would like a few days to take a close look at your offer, just to make sure I'm really clear on its details. Is it okay if I call you in the meantime if I have any additional questions?"

If you think you truly do have other offers pending, use this offer to graciously let the other companies know that you are now considering an opportunity. This is what you say:

"I'm in some discussions with a company that has extended an opportunity to me that I have to take into very serious consideration. But I've also been very interested in our conversations as well, so I was wondering if you had a sense of timing on your decision? I can probably defer this company for a short while, but not for very long. What's your sense of how things stand on your end?"

You're not unnecessarily rushing or pushing anyone to make a decision before they have to or want to. You're just giving every one fair warning that if they want you, now's the time to turn their conversations with you into a real offer.

The best thing you can do:
Keep your funnel full of suspects, prospects, opportunities, and targets until you have officially accepted the offer of your choice. Even then, make sure you continue networking throughout your career.

The worst thing you can do:
Pin all your hopes on one offer and lose control of the decision-making process.

The first thing you should do:
Keep in mind that just because you haven't heard from the hiring manager, that doesn't mean he's not interested.

Be Ready to Walk Away

Inez was getting fed up, to put it mildly. She had the best possible referral into her dream company: the chairman himself. That should have generated an avalanche of return phone calls and eager invitations for meetings. It didn't. It generated just another round of frustrations. The chairman's employees would dutifully reach out to her, suggest she name a few dates and times for appointments. But then, they never confirmed the suggested meeting time. After months of fruitless attempts, her connection to the company withered from neglect—not to mention her interest in working with that company after all.

Her frustration progressed to the point of annoyance. What kind of people would blow off the chairman? But she was still in control of her temper and dignity. So, she tried one more last-ditch effort, which was to walk away. She wrote a final email to the middle manager who was supposed to meet with her saying, "This is a quick follow-up to my email offering a couple of times for us to meet. I assume that you weren't able to confirm our suggested appointment times because other priorities have captured your attention or you do not wish to move forward at this time. Unfortunately, I wasn't able to keep those suggested times open. And now my calendar is pretty much booked for the rest of the month. Here's hoping that one day we will have the opportunity to meet. In the meantime, have a good summer."

The neglectful manager returned her email within the hour, apologizing, and requesting a firm appointment the first week of the following month.

In reviewing what just happened, Inez could only guess what triggered the change: "I was really ready to let this company go. And it became a matter of my own self-respect more than anything. As much as I needed them to know that my availability wasn't to be taken for granted, it was also important for me to remember that I still deserved to be treated with respect. I guess they got the message, too."

CHAPTER 28

Collaborate on Creating Your Job Description

Throughout this book, we've been highlighting all the advantages to be found in the hidden job market (HJM) and the practical ways you can leverage them to advance your job search. Control. Speed. Efficiency. Economy. Reduced competition, if any. Focus.

But we saved this one till the end: You can do more to write your own ticket in the hidden job market than the traditional "respond to the published job ad" job. You can open almost any possibilities you want in your new HJM job. You just have to write that ticket in a language that your hiring manager can understand.

This is when thinking like a manager takes on a whole new level of importance. You will be custom writing your own job specifications in collaboration with your hiring manager. Because the two of you are working together to whip up this new job, you are in the perfect position to help the hiring manager help you. And you do that by first making sure you understand exactly what the hiring manager actually needs from you once you're in that position.

As the hiring manager has begun to warm up to the idea of actually bringing you onboard, she hasn't been obsessing about "Gee, how can we help this person with a job?" (You wouldn't want to be hired under those circumstances anyway. You're not a charity case.) What's on her mind is the perfectly legitimate question: "How can this person help me in our work and help the organization be more successful?"

The answer is found in at least one of three categories of the hiring manager's mindset:

- **The need to increase revenue.** What role would you play in bringing in new customers? Opening new markets? Adding a new service? Finding a new funding source? Creating new technology? Bringing existing technology to a new industry, market or product? Finding fresh way to market the company's goods and services?

- **The need to reduce costs.** How might you help reduce costs by improving processes? Increasing efficiencies? Retaining talent? Improving safety practices? Improving information flow?

- **The need to shift the workload.** If your new hiring manager gave you work that another member of her staff does, that might free them up to take on a new task. Or, your hiring manager has probably watched her own job morph over recent months and years. And, over time, she has taken on responsibilities that she would love to delegate to someone else … to someone like you, for instance! This way, she can turn her attention to high-value business concerns that are closer to her own AMF sweet spot.

So, when you start the conversation with managers about what you might be able to do for them, don't just unfurl a long list of possibilities (any of which they might reject). Instead, ask *them* what *they* want. That question can be asked straight out. Or you can finesse it a little bit.

> "What issues or projects would be on top of your priority list for the next person you hire?"

> "How is your team measured, and which metrics would you like to improve with your next hire?"

> "What situations would you want someone like me to manage or be responsible for?"

Your goal at this point is to understand the core drivers of that company, that division, or that department's business. The justification for hiring you will be an economic justification. But that doesn't mean that you must abandon your search for meaningful work. You just need to be able to tie a market value to what you do. For instance, you say your dream job is to save puppies by finding responsible homes for adoption? Great. Find an organization where puppy saving is a core reason for being in existence. The job itself, though, must be somehow connected to the economics of the organization: raising money to save puppies or saving more puppies for less money. Or doing such a fantastic job lobbying for spay/neuter programs that the organization's members happily renew their annual dues. Somewhere in the mix of any and every job description lies a financial consideration. That's life.

Regardless of the job, the answers to these questions are the starting point where you and your hiring manager can begin writing the job description with this proposition: "This is where you might be able to help me."

As you exchange ideas about what the *solution* looks like—not necessarily an actual job—jot down the notes of the key points of pain that your presence could be the solution for. What kind of pain? Pain for hiring managers might be a problem, or a challenge that they're dealing with, or an opportunity that they might think they're missing. Then, when the time is right (when the flow of ideas dwindles), say, "Let's take a moment to summarize what we've just talked about. Here's what I'm hearing you say. You want this, this, this, this, and this."

When the hiring manager confirms your summary, if it still appeals to you as a potential job description, say, "That sounds very interesting to me. How can we formalize this?" Your hiring manager will get the idea. It's not so much that you're literally writing down a job description as you are having a conversation about what the components are—all from the perspective of what your hiring manager is looking for.

If you have the impression that the job, as it's been brainstormed so far, is a little too far down the org chart to suit your ambition, this is the time to try to move it into a higher job classification, with more responsibility. These questions will help you gauge where the prospective job will be positioned in the influence hierarchy:

> "For this role, who would be my peers? Who would you see as the key stakeholders?"
>
> "For this job to function at its highest potential, what would the reporting structure look like?"
>
> "If what you're looking for is accountability to deliver on these objectives, should the people who provide the different components report to and be responsible to the person who has that accountability?"

If you have been in management, you know that reporting structures, responsibility, and resources are keys to success. Discuss these issues with the hiring manager. Not just in terms of job titles and hierarchy, but also in terms of objectives, decision-making authority, and resources. Your input can influence decisions about what the job looks like.

In contrast, when a job description is written by the staffing department, it's not written with you and your talents in mind. It becomes a rather bloodless list of requirements set against a matrix of organizational strategies and objectives.

But when you are able to co-author your job description with your hiring manager, dovetailing their wants and needs with your own AMF, you don't just have a list. You have a story—a story of how your service to the company can directly serve its core objectives. And how you can really make life a whole lot easier for your boss. And how you are the one they should hire for the job.

The best thing you can do:
Define what your job might ultimately look like by inviting the hiring manager to brainstorm with you.

The worst thing you can do:
Ask about pay, benefits, or vacation time when you're still writing the job specifications.

The first thing you should do:
Ask your boss a variety of questions based on this theme: What do you want that you don't have now?

Pets and P&L

Carol started her working life as thousands of other youngsters do—as a barista for a national coffee retail chain. But in addition to focusing only on the intricacies of all the different coffee drinks, she also paid attention to the intricacies of small store operations. She loved watching how the slightest changes in small store management could directly benefit the business. Over the years, she moved up the corporate ladder of a company that sells smoothies and juices, until one day, the company changed its business model and she was out of work. This was her chance to reassess her priorities, passions, and abilities.

She saw that while her professional passions still focused on P&L, her personal passions involved pets and their needs. As luck would have it, one of the major national pet retailers was headquartered near her home. But, unfortunately, it was laying people off and had a hiring freeze. But, strictly in the spirit of running an HJM research meeting, Carol reached out to one of the operations executives and asked for an appointment.

During the meeting, the executive disclosed that the company was experimenting with a new business model that would involve small, upscale urban shops—a setting that she was uniquely expert in! Very quickly, the meeting turned into a discussion about what kind of team she would need to help the company launch the new store concept successfully. She helped them define not only her own position, title, and role, but also what other kinds of players the company needed to make this small store happen.

Within six months, the company successfully opened its first small store and defined a new market niche in which it had no competitors.

If Carol had been discouraged from approaching the company because it had a hiring freeze and was actually laying people off, she never would have had the chance to help the company change its business model. The company may have been reducing its staff, but its executives wisely spotted the company's future in Carol and snapped her up.

CHAPTER 29

Negotiating Your New Job

When you're in an HJM research meeting that morphs into an actual full-blown job interview, the subject of money is bound to come up. Compensation negotiations might seem a little trickier in the hidden job market arena, because if there is no posted job to begin with, there's no posted salary range either. So, you might have the feeling that you're trying to get numbers-specific in a vast landscape where no one really has any data to use as a starting point. The answer "I dunno, what do you think?" just won't cut it.

Because you've begun the conversation in an informal, unofficial meeting, you have several variables working in your favor:

You've probably bypassed the whole HR "we won't let you past reception until you fill out this application *completely*" thing. So, many companies want to know what your previous salary was before they'll even take your coat. Since you were not yet officially applying for a job, you're already comfortably seated in the hiring manager's office brainstorming all the wonderful possibilities of what a role for you would look like. Result: You're not tied to your last pitiful salary and the meager 10% they might be willing to offer you to bring you onboard.

Because your HJM research meeting has morphed into a job interview, by the time money comes up, the hiring manager is starting to get emotionally attached to the idea of having you join the company. You don't have to sell yourself by being the cheapest candidate in the bunch. You've already begun selling yourself based on the value that you're bringing to the organization. The two of you are now a team, collaborating to figure out a way that *"we* can make this thing happen." If you have a salary expectation that's a little higher than what the hiring manager prefers, he is going to weigh the value and economy of having you onboard now, versus spending as much as 30% of your salary more in delays and expense while they try to find a cheaper version of you. You could be perfect. You're not asking for the moon *and* the stars. And you're there. Why not just hire you instead?

Budgets are flexible. Your target company may not have seen you coming, so it might not have an actual job description with an actual salary attached to it. If they want you badly enough, they'll probably be able to find the money—especially if your presence in the company represents money saved or generated in other ways. If your hiring manager says, "We don't have the budget for this position," that just opens up another line of discussion, starting with you finding a way to diplomatically ask, "Who owns the budget for this kind of initiative and so might see the value?"

The beauty of the hidden job market is that you're less likely to be boxed in by any of the policy or budget barriers that candidates for posted job openings must contend with. And, because you've come in through the proverbial back door, your competition is less— if it exists at all. So, the conversation about your compensation expectations isn't confounded by the possibility that Candidate B might be 5% cheaper in terms of salary expectation.

Still, as with any compensation discussion, this is a sensitive phase of your conversation with the hiring manager. How you conduct it will demonstrate not only how much you want the job, but also how much you value yourself (therefore how much the company should value you), what kind of businessperson you are, and how nicely you play ball with others, even when something as important as money is at stake. Not negotiating is not an option. To simply accept what's offered would probably result in being paid thousands of dollars less throughout the lifetime of your career with this organization. So negotiate with calm, focus, and graciousness. Once you say yes, the negotiation is over. And your relationship with the company as an employee has begun.

Don't get caught up in a compensation discussion too soon. If your HJM meeting partner wants to know what your last salary was before you sense an imminent offer, he may be trying to gauge what kind of salary offer to extend based on your past (hello, Mr. 10%). Or he might be more interested in what you cost rather than what you're going to be worth to the organization. If you start the conversation already too expensive, you won't have the chance to finish it to anyone's satisfaction. If you lowball yourself, you've doomed your prospects of ever snagging that potential salary jump. There is no reason your next compensation structure should be based on your last salary, especially if you're about to take on a totally different job, at a totally different company, with a totally different compensation structure.

You want to be cooperative, but you don't want to be forthcoming, not quite yet. So say something like, "I've always been paid in the upper range of my peers. And the packages I'm currently evaluating have many components, beyond simple salary. So, let's get into the specifics once we determine that there's really a fit between your company's needs and my skills." You're not being coy, you're just staying in control of your side of the conversation. And it signals to them that you are willing to defer gratification and that you're not going to leap at just any old offer.

If that doesn't work, and you're feeling that you're still being pressed to rush the process (before you're confident that they really want you), simply say, "I appreciate that you want to know what I made in my last position because it will tell you whether we should continue to discuss this job. Tell me what the range is for this particular position, and if it doesn't appear to be a fit, I will certainly withdraw my candidacy and not waste either of our time. We both want this to be a great fit for both sides." You're being collaborative, not adversarial.

Eventually, though, you will have to settle into a conversation about compensation—when and only when you and the hiring manager have agreed that working together is a very exciting prospect for both of you.

Come equipped with salary data, which you have collected from your previous HJM research meetings. One of the benefits of HJM research meetings is that you get to ask those kinds of questions without looking like you're desperate for a job with that particular company. Once you start getting really interested in a particular company, it's more difficult to ask those kinds of questions in a casual, detached way. In the job interview itself, share that information with your hiring manager, saying, "This is what I've seen in the salaries that are out there right now, so this is the neighborhood of the compensation I would be expecting. How does this look to you? Does it fit with what your compensation plan looks like?"

Keep in mind that the company's compensation strategy could reveal something about its position in the market and what kind of coworkers you might have. Ask the question, "What is your compensation strategy? What percentile of the market do you want to be in?" If the hiring manager says, "We want to be in the middle of the market," that tells you that their performance expectations might be average as well. If they say that they want to keep their compensation structure below market, that may signal to you that your coworkers might be mediocre or that you'll be dealing with a team suffering from high turnover (if you stick around long yourself). Likewise, if they pay above market, you might be working with some exciting people who are doing industry-leading stuff.

Don't let your passion for the job cause you to sell yourself short. It's not any easier to get a job because you're offering yourself at below market. In fact, it's just as difficult, if not harder. Wise hiring managers will know if they're getting you at a "fire sale" price, and they'll keep in mind that your motivation might start to flag as soon as the immediate financial urgency is behind you. Is your family going to be happy with you, if you have to impose budget cutbacks because you couldn't hold out for what you deserve? Will you be distracted at work by the dissatisfaction at home? You're going to have a hard time convincing a wise hiring manager that you'd be happy for less just to have a chance at the job.

That said, don't overlook the value of nonmonetary negotiable and compensation, such as an extra week's paid time off (which, if you value free time as much as cash in hand, could equate to 2% of your salary), or even memberships to airline clubs, if you will travel a great deal for business. Also, include in those discussions items related to the job itself, budget for staffing, and tools to do the job, such as computers, memberships, and conference fees. Smart negotiators always position such requests as benefits to the company because they will help them do their job better for the company. These negotiation strategies can be used for any job offer, but when the position was never published, they often are not subject to a set of pre-established conditions decided before the first interview.

The best thing you can do:
Put off entering into the negotiations process until after they have shown they are sincerely interested in hiring you and want to make you an offer.

The worst thing you can do:
Say yes to the position before you settle on terms. Once you say yes, negotiations are over.

The first thing you should do:
Make sure that you get salary information in as many HJM research meetings as possible so that you can eventually get the best possible deal for yourself when the real interviews start.

Why Wait for the Raise?

When Bob lost his job as an IT manager at a bank, he realized that he was happy in IT but didn't want to be a manager anymore. He was through with managing other people. He just wanted to do the work he enjoyed, which was simply IT work. This meant less pay; he was aware of that. His willingness to climb down a few rungs of the organizational ladder confused hiring managers, who were used to applicants wanting to negotiate up, not willing to negotiate down.

After a round of interviews, Bob was offered a job with a software company. The hiring manager said, "I'd like to pay you what you're really worth, but it would be at the very top of the range for this position posting. And then, I wouldn't be able to give you raises. So, my offer is just slightly above the midpoint of the range. This will give us head room for raises in the next two years."

Bob thought that the idea of a couple of raises in the foreseeable future was really enticing. But then, he thought again: Why not take the top of the pay range now instead? It would mean giving up the raises, true. But instead, he would be making more money now.

So, he broached the idea to his hiring manager, acknowledging that he would be foregoing raises in the upcoming months. And he confirmed that he will understand when the time came and he was passed over. The hiring manager saw the logic of Bob's thinking. And agreed.

Result? Bob raised his starting salary by $7,000.

You Have What It Takes to Get the Right Job

Now that you're almost finished with this book, you have probably noticed that the hidden job market requires action, energy, stamina, creativity, and initiative to land your next job. Which, as far as we're concerned, is much better than all the *waiting* that's required of you in the passive, published job market. We promised to show you a set of job search techniques that will absolutely put you in the driver's seat. But the rub is that now you're the one who has to do the driving if you want to make the hidden job market work for you.

So, you have to put yourself out there. A lot. And if you're one of those people who has thought of themselves as shy or introverted since high school, you might think, "Oh great, and the advantage, once again, goes to the cool kids."

Sure, it might be easier for the extroverted to motivate themselves to actually get out of the house. But the distinction stops there. In his nearly 18 years of counseling clients in their job search, Duncan saw that extroverted and introverted people succeeded equally in the hidden job market. And, although it might have been easier for the extroverts to pick up the phone and make the initial cold calls, Duncan saw that some of the best techniques and ideas came from the clients who were quiet, methodical, and thoughtful about the way they approached their work and many aspects of their life overall.

As it turns out, succeeding in the job market has less to do with your innate social talents and more to do with how to manage your time and energy—as well as the integrity you bring to the whole process. So, here is our final list for you, the essential ingredients to personally drive a successful HJM search campaign.

These "ingredients" have nothing to do with how outgoing you are; instead, they depend on your attitude and discipline and the commitment you bring to finding the job that's right for you.

Successful HJM job searchers…

- **Treat this project as a full-time job.** According to the Bureau of Labor Statistics, the average jobseeker spends only 1.7 hours a day looking (as opposed to looking *and* worrying) for work. Perhaps it's because they don't know how to do more than two hours' worth of investigating every day. Or they're trusting the so-called system to fetch them job interviews like a golden retriever. With the hidden job market, there is always plenty of productive work to do. So, *you'll* never be at a loss as to how to fill up a full workweek. But just as important, you can give yourself the evenings and weekends off (which is essential to sustaining your stamina and avoiding burnout).

- **Approach the job search with a high degree of integrity.** Your networking is authentic. You have the confidence to know that eventually the right opportunities will come around, so you can be upfront about looking for a job without feeling like you are begging for work. You are able to stay dignified and engaged in the HJM job search process, remembering that when the match is right, it will benefit your new employer as much as it will bring some level of security back into your life.

- **Pass on leads and opportunities to others.** You don't want to get so caught up in helping other people on their job search that you neglect your own journey. But on the other hand, because you're out there in circulation, you will uncover needs, issues, and opportunities that could be perfect for someone else. Someone you know.

- **Engage in constant learning.** One mistake that jobseekers often make is that they assume that they know everything they need to know about how they fit in their profession and industry. But your skills can be used in industries that you haven't even thought of before. When you had your last full-time job, you knew how important it was to be constantly updating your skills, coming up with new ideas, staying on top of your market trends, and so forth. That hasn't changed. While you're searching the hidden job market, your ongoing curiosity will drive you to learning about new companies and surprising new ways your skills can be used. Your curiosity will override any shyness you might feel when facing the prospect of meeting new people. And you'll be constantly building your capabilities and attractiveness to employers.

- **Stay adaptable and flexible.** The job search and the job search marketplace is a really messy, disorganized affair. No matter how systematic your own approach is, HJM meetings and interviews can get postponed or canceled. That person you thought would be a fantastic connection turned out to be a dud. Then, you make a valuable connection completely by chance when your job search is the last thing on your mind, and because you are better prepared, you leverage it into your next opportunity. That's the mystery of the process.

- **Have a sense of humor.** Sometimes, you just have to laugh.

- **Are open-minded.** You increase your chances of serendipitous connections if you stay open to all possibilities and people. Be willing to be surprised by unexpected sources of inspiration, dubious sources of job leads, and some crazy introductions. If you hold the belief that there are some people you should talk to and others who probably aren't worth the time and effort, you're drastically limiting your possibilities.

- **Are organized.** Granted, some people are more naturally talented at organization than others. But you can set up a system that works for you. Make sure your system supports your commitment to follow up with all your networking contacts at least three times.

- **Trust the process.** Keep your spirits up by celebrating the small successes along the way. The day is successful if you are given new referrals to contact; if you learn something new; if you get to tell your story to new people; if you show your TOP to someone who can help fill in a few more empty spaces with names and contact information. It's a successful day if you're able to overcome fear and temptation and say no to a job offer that's not right for you. And it's a really successful day when you're offered just the right job with just the right terms.

You are about to embark on one of the most challenging journeys of your life. As you go through the process, you'll learn about yourself as much as you'll discover new career prospects in your field, industry, or community. You will make connections and build relationships that will stay with you throughout your entire career, if not your life.

The hidden job market will be satisfying, nerve-wracking, worrisome, exciting, inspiring, exasperating, and amazing. There might be days when you can't seem to make progress no matter how hard you try. And then, suddenly, you're filling your calendar with intriguing appointments. You're discovering that you have much more control than you would have ever thought.

When you're facing those moments when it feels like you're in a never-ending tunnel of frustration, take heart. One of these days, you will hear, "We would like to make you an offer."

It will happen.

Why We Wrote This Book

Duncan

I grew up in Seattle and graduated from college at the height of the Boeing layoffs. Unemployment exceeded 10%, and in 1971, when the slump was at its worst, someone put up a billboard near the airport that read, *"Will the last person leaving Seattle please turn out the lights?"** My dad was a dedicated Boeing employee, and during that time, he thought that each week would be his last in a profession he loved: designing, as he was fond of calling them, "flying machines." He survived the cutbacks, but no one in our family ever breathed easily about job security again. Many of his friends lost their jobs despite their considerable skills and talents. It was a lousy time to graduate from college, but a good time to learn how to take control of a job search.

Later, in the '90s, I found my calling in the "outplacement" industry, working with companies and their employees as they went through painful downsizings that pushed unemployment close to double digits in Southern California. Week after week, I would meet people typically on the day they lost their job. Some were relieved, others were angry, many were teary, but most were simply stunned. As the realization of their job loss sunk in, they knew that they had the daunting task of finding a new job. Most of my clients were highly accomplished in their careers. Some were burned out; others were trapped in a dead end or train wreck of a career that did not match what they did

---

* My apologies to the Seattle Chamber of Commerce for bringing up *that* painful historical tidbit.

best. It wasn't their fault that they had derailed long before they were actually let go. I knew, as did my colleagues at the firm, that the best jobs did not go to the best people. Rather, the best jobs went to those who were best at the job search—particularly when the job market was tight.

When I started in the outplacement business, most companies hired us to work with their ex-employees until they found a job—regardless of the economy, regardless of their profession, their age, or where they lived. My clients looked to me to give them the creative ideas, resources, advice, and tools for their job search. And if my ideas did not work, they were in my office the next week anxiously asking, "Now what should I do?" This was a serious question. The welfare of people's families was on the line.

Mortgages still had to be paid, kids sent to college, and the nest egg protected from being wiped out from a job search that outlasted the meager company severance package.

Fast forward almost 20 years. The job market once again looks just painful for the unemployed, and we are reminded that job security can quickly evaporate in a matter of weeks—creating yet another new army of career refugees. As a result, published job openings are swamped with applications. Competition is tough. Talented people are trying to land new jobs. But they are routinely told they are overqualified, underqualified, or not qualified at all.

There has to be a better way. And, in fact, there is. This is the reason why we wrote this book. It's time for you to benefit from this approach that I developed though my work with clients who gave me their best ideas and who challenged me to come up with better ones. While this approach can be used in pursuit of any published job posting, it is particularly effective with jobs that are never advertised or posted online, or in other words, jobs that make up the "hidden job market."

These tools and techniques are practical, to the point, and tested in the real world by my clients and myself, as throughout my own career, I have successfully changed professions from non-profit to profit, small companies to large companies, and from highly technical software products to management consulting. Life is too short and interesting for one career.

Martha

As with Duncan, I was raised by a father who loved his work. But he couldn't talk about it to his family, like Duncan's dad could. He was a covert operative for the Central Intelligence Agency. His job: to recruit spies in such Cold War hot spots as Cuba, Berlin, Saigon, Mexico City, Vienna, and Madrid. Although he didn't speak of it at the dinner table (whenever he was actually home for dinner), there was no doubt that my dad found his calling and devoted his life to it.

Unlike Duncan's dad, my dad got laid off. (How do you lay off a spy? I guess the same way you lay anyone off—with a pink slip and an expression of sincere regret.) And so, Duncan and I found our first commonality in the fact that it was our fathers' respective professional crises that deeply affected our own out-look on the career world. And our fathers' experiences handed us our own callings.

While Duncan devoted his energies to the outplacement world on the West Coast, I became a journalist on the East Coast, singularly focused on the questions about what makes work, work. We didn't know each other then. But we were destined to meet. And I'm so glad we did.

In our professional and personal lives, we have witnessed the pain and joy that come with people losing their jobs and then regaining their footing on their professional paths again. And this book helps you regain your footing as you go through your search for your next job. It's not enough to just find a gig that pays the bills. You deserve better than that. And it's our desire that the book you hold in your hands will introduce you to a proven system that will help you find and land the job that's absolutely right for you.

Unlock the Hidden Job Market is about job search when the job search is tough. It's tougher today because there are fewer published positions and more competition. It's tougher because you might be forced to ditch what you have done in the past and transfer your hard-won skills to new industries and professions. It's tougher because you have higher expectations for your career happiness—but perhaps lower levels of trust that you can count on your employer to give you that happiness. Because the challenges are so much tougher now, shouldn't the results of your hard work be even more rewarding for your efforts? That's what we want for you.

We wrote this book to help you reach beyond the limits of the published job market to the really great jobs that are out there waiting for you. Even in a tough job market.

When can you start?

Index

FT Press
FINANCIAL TIMES

In an increasingly competitive world, it is quality
of thinking that gives an edge—an idea that opens new
doors, a technique that solves a problem, or an insight
that simply helps make sense of it all.

We work with leading authors in the various arenas
of business and finance to bring cutting-edge thinking
and best-learning practices to a global market.

It is our goal to create world-class print publications
and electronic products that give readers
knowledge and understanding that can then be
applied, whether studying or at work.

To find out more about our business
products, you can visit us at www.ftpress.com.